Avoiders

*How They Become
and Remain Depressed*

Michael A. Church, Ph. D.

authorHOUSE®

AuthorHouse™
1663 Liberty Drive
Bloomington, IN 47403
www.authorhouse.com
Phone: 1 (800) 839-8640

Published by AuthorHouse 11/03/2016

ISBN: 978-1-5246-4663-9 (sc)
ISBN: 978-1-5246-4664-6 (hc)
ISBN: 978-1-5246-4662-2 (e)

Library of Congress Control Number: 2016917699

Print information available on the last page.

Any people depicted in stock imagery provided by Thinkstock are models, and such images are being used for illustrative purposes only. Certain stock imagery © *Thinkstock.*

This book is printed on acid-free paper.

Table of Contents

Acknowledgements

There are several people the author would like to thank for their help with this book. First and foremost, Dominique Church was instrumental in helping design the presentation of the conceptual framework of the text. Her editorial comments were truly insightful and creative. I appreciate her editorial comments too, along with those provided by Trina Butler. Also, thanks are extended to Natasha Rostova for her help with some of the typing and computer layout, as well as Liz Blaskiewicz for aid with final editing of the manuscript. Lastly, special thanks are expressed to Nelya Church, my wife, who understood the time commitment this project required and supported me throughout. She is undoubtedly a model for the power of acceptance in promoting positive intrapersonal development and interpersonal relationships.

Dedication

This book is dedicated to Psychology, the professional love of my life. I feel so blessed to have been able to have a career in such an interesting, expanding and useful field. Every work day has been unique, challenging and full of endless possibilities; some more so than others of course. Psychology has afforded me the opportunity to grow as a person while finding purpose in educating and helping others. I have been guided by the thought that, even after I am gone, the people I have influenced can continue to pass on whatever constructive and positive lessons they have learned. Because Psychology is so complex and comprehensive, it has never been boring and afforded me the latitude to explore changing interests and values. As I have gotten older, so too have my clients. We continue to collaborate in an endless flow of learning about ourselves as we evolve. I have had the opportunity to engage in activities such as individual psychotherapy with people throughout the life span, group and family therapy, hypnosis, forensic evaluations, and serve as a preceptor for medical students and as a panel member for UNAI, a body of the United Nations, on the impact of education on women. These are just some of the highlights of a career I never imagined would be so rich in purpose and meaning. I feel so fortunate to have made the choice to jump on the train of Psychology just as it was picking up so much momentum in being so interesting and relevant in our societies.

Preface

For many decades, psychology has focused a great deal of attention on the power of positive reinforcement. Articles, books, talk shows, self-improvement classes, parenting, employee relations, advertisement, education, etc. frequently expose the importance of rewarding constructive behavior. These developments are certainly understandable and have been beneficial in helping individuals, couples, groups and organizations function in more positive and satisfying ways. It is clear that approval, recognition, medals, praise, tokens, money and other forms of positive reinforcement have powerful and lasting effects on helping people acquire skills, act appropriately and maintain responsible behavior patterns. However, a main thesis of this book is that we have over-sold positive reinforcement. In doing so we have failed to recognize the powerful role of negative reinforcement which involves the relief felt when we avoid or escape from unpleasant experiences.

The power of negative reinforcement can be seen daily via the liberal and effective use of it in our society. Examples include interest penalties for not paying bills on time, being fired for not showing on time or for work, a lower grade for not turning in homework, prison terms for not following parole or probation guidelines, being ticketed for not stopping fully at a stop sign, etc. Naturally, we try to avoid or escape from these types of consequences. Note that these situations are externally imposed by some organization or person(s). What about situations where we are the person who both delivers and receives negative reinforcement? Examples include feeling a sense of relief when we circumvent or run from stress, tell a lie, cheat on an exam, withdraw from others via excessive use of computers and phone apps, use drugs or alcohol to blunt negative thoughts or emotions, etc. The reader will see how these types of self-induced patterns of avoidance and escape lead to chronic depression and/or other psychological problems. This is the type of coping pattern which characterizes the Avoider. Avoiders routinely shove important stressors, obligations, responsibilities and realities under the rug which almost inevitably causes problems to mount to a point where they become demoralized and overwhelmed. Eventually, they are likely to feel disgusted with themselves, their lifestyle and relationships and other stressors, leading them to feel chronically discontent and be labeled a "depressed" person." Note that this label is not an explanation but simply a description. Moreover, with people who are chronically depressed, it is employed even when there has not been any great loss, trauma or extreme stressors (i.e., despite the fact that they have essentially been their own worst enemy). Along this vein, depression is not viewed as the main target or problem. Rather, depression is the side effect of the core problem; that is, excessive and inappropriate patterns of avoiding unpleasant behaviors and thoughts. Interestingly, this type of depression is viewed as a natural consequence of patterns of avoidance because most people would be depressed if they were living the life of an Avoider.

This book is not a referendum on the use of positive versus negative consequences to influence and control of human behavior. Rather, it is written to highlight how patterns of avoidance as coping styles create and sustain chronic depression, as well as other psychological disorders. To put it bluntly, it is about how avoidance forces can cause us to retreat into a black hole. It is also about what can be done to help prevent or get ourselves out of such a state. The concept of Avoider is introduced in this book and refers to individuals who display relatively stable and self-defeating styles of running from various forms of stress, thereby making them vulnerable to chronic psychological disorder(s). This concept is based on research performed by the author on over 1200 individuals for more than a decade, as well as a wealth of clinical, research, teaching and anecdotal life experiences. Review of available books failed to turn up a single one on the concept of Avoider. Numerous research articles on avoidance were available, as well as ones on the avoidant personality. In addition, a few books on the avoidant personality disorder could be found. Thus, there are some works associated with the concept of Avoider that have been integrated within this book.

This book was written to highlight the concept of Avoider as a wake-up call to the power of avoidance forces in our lives. It is hoped that it can serve as an integrative tool that can be utilized in how we view and communicate about (and with) people who over-utilize avoidance as a coping mechanism and lifestyle.

Although no particular theory or type of therapeutic application underscores this book, it is slanted toward a relatively contemporary type of conceptual framework, namely Acceptance and Commitment Therapy (ACT). ACT-related approaches are part of a "third wave" of cognitive-behavioral theory/therapy which has been gaining significantly in popularity during the past 15-20 years, largely because of its effectiveness in treating chronic and complex cases of psychological disorders. ACT principles and theory seem to fit well into the concept of Avoiders and are used frequently to underscore interpretations and conclusions put forth by this author. At the same time, more traditional treatment approaches will be discussed in terms of how they can be used alternatively or in combination with the third wave.

This book is designed primarily for lay persons as a self-help book, although it may serve also as a foundation for many who are about to enter therapy or are already engaged in this process. In other words, it is written to provide a supplement for people who are considering therapy or may desire a way to speed up their recovery process, as well as for people who may want to attempt self-help as opposed to, or prior to considering, formal psychiatric or psychological treatment. It is not a "how to" book per se. Although specific treatment priorities and recommendations will be advanced, the human mind is too complex to offer straightforward "fixes." On the contrary, this book will explicate important factors related to psychological difficulties and the treatments that can be beneficial without making claims that the steps involved are analogous to fixing a car or computer. Clinicians and clients will need to sort through the material presented herein and creatively piece together what works best for them, as it is not a one size fits all approach. It is also written for students in psychology who are taking courses at various levels. Many of the ACT-type books available are written for the professional or graduate student in psychology. They tend to be conceptually challenging and "wordy." This book has intentionally been written at a level designed for the nonprofessional, although counselors, psychiatrists and social workers may benefit from reading it too. The conceptual framework presented herein offers some unique perspectives which professionals may find useful in their practice. It is geared also to the practitioner who wants a straightforward, basic approach to material that can be very challenging to grasp, even for the seasoned professional. The author hopes that you find this book helpful in whatever ways desired.

Chapter One

The Power of Avoidance Forces

Do you ever question why there are so many people taking antidepressant medication, many of whom seem to have pretty good lives? Do you wonder why some people linger with depression for so long, even though they have taken numerous medications? And, why do you think that some people bounce back from depression so well while others don't get up from what seems to be relatively weak blows? These and other related questions should not seem so vague and difficult to understand after reading this book. It took a very long time for medicine to abandon the idea that fever, bleeding, coughing, etc., were not the disease process. So too, psychology is now focusing more on the core causes of psychological distress and disorders, as opposed to symptoms such as depression. Although it is certainly tempting to view depression, anxiety, eating disorders, gambling and drug/alcohol abuse and other psychological problems as the "illness," more careful and closer examination reveals that these psychological difficulties are usually associated with consistent underlying causations, particularly patterns of avoidance and escape. In other words, these disorders are typically "side effects" of maladaptive coping styles inherent in personality functioning. The importance of this distinction cannot be underestimated because it guides how we interpret and treat various psychological problems. When we simplistically see symptoms as the psychological problem, there is a tendency to resort to short-term palliative treatments while failing to focus on core causations of the so-called disorder(s). We may view the gambler or alcoholic as a victim of being born with a disease. Or, we may simply see the sufferer as having to cope with genetically driven anxiety or

1

depression which permanently affects their functioning, and is best treated with medication. Some might even view the depressed person as lacking the courage to change or adapt constructively. These orientations may not only help undermine responsibility and active coping on the part of the sufferer but, at the same time, suggest that superficial answers are the most appropriate way to perceive them. At best, medication is a general approach to specific problems and treats symptoms (Church & Brooks, 2010). Does anyone really believe that psychiatric medication goes to specific areas of the brain and fixes, repairs or adjusts the neurons or brain centers involved in various behavior problems? Moreover, medication often fails to produce positive effects and/or causes negative ones (e.g., side effects) while leaving the underlying cause(s) unexposed. Frequently, symptoms return when medication is curtailed.

A symptom-disease approach tends to be appealing to many physicians, patients, family members, and even some insurance and pharmaceutical companies. It seems cheaper in the short-run, convenient, tends to relieve feelings of responsibility on the part of the sufferer, offers a quick fix approach to the wishful thinker, and promises less effort up front. We know that insurance companies are under intense pressure to show profitability in the short run, leaving them less and less concerned about what is in the in the best long-term interest of the patient. Sadly, it often leaves the patient suffering with subpar and narrowly focused treatments. More to the point, treatment of effects rather than causes is likely to be superficial at best and, at worst, leads to more intense feelings of helplessness, hopelessness and demoralization while delaying treatment targeted at underlying causes of their problem(s). In some cases this type of ineffectiveness may even help facilitate suicide ideation and/or behavior (Church and Brooks, 2009).

After performing individual and group psychotherapy for several decades with people suffering from depression and many other psychological disorders, it became evident that traditional cognitive-behavioral psychotherapy was only minimally effective with some clients, particularly those suffering from chronic psychological disorders. Simply getting clients to substitute more rational and constructive thoughts and behaviors for presumably distorted, illogical or self-defeating ones was often ineffective or only yielded partial positive changes.

We are all aware of the power of motivation in both causing and sustaining our behavior patterns. We all experience the motivational conflict of both been drawn toward (approach) and away from (avoid) a goal or outcome. Clearly, we cannot obtain our desired outcomes when we are unable to approach and complete goal-directed behaviors. If this type of behavior pattern becomes consistent, then we are almost assured of being dissatisfied. Of course, it seems reasonable to ask why a person capable of logical and rational thought would routinely avoid seeking important goals. Fortunately, there is relevant research bearing on this question, some old and some new. Many decades ago, Dollard and Miller (1950) demonstrated that, as we get closer to a goal object, avoidance forces accelerate in strength faster than approach forces. The resulting effect of this phenomenon is that we may "chicken out" just prior to engaging in goal directed behavior, even in the face of something greatly desired. Another relevant and related research finding is that unpleasant events tend to be more powerful than pleasant ones (Baumeister, et. al., 2001). For example, it is been estimated that, generally speaking, for most people winning $1000 has about the same emotional intensity as losing $200. Thus, it becomes easy to see why we may be hesitant to approach goals that are associated with negative emotions, such as anxiety and fear. Although we have a strong desire to obtain certain goals, we can be overwhelmed by the anticipation of unpleasant feelings (e.g., anxiety) of stressful (e.g., fear) or painful events. To place this conceptual framework in another context, although we are social animals who desire affection and intimacy, the anxiety and fear related to rejection, embarrassment and/or disapproval renders many of us to loneliness, alienation and withdrawal. It is, of course, understandable that we usually try to avoid the unpleasantness caused by psychological and physical pain. Moreover, avoidance of pain is wired into our biology because it tends to enhance survival potential. Thus, we naturally tend to avoid fire, things that smell and taste horrible, people who could harm us, etc. However, when patterns of avoidance are inappropriate and/or excessive, the probability of psychological maladjustment increases and survival potential may very well decrease. Clearly, we need to know when it is imperative to confront painful experiences, even when our natural propensity is to avoid or escape (e.g., surgery). As will become clear, realistic confrontation of life stressors generally leads to development of better adaptive skills, more self-confidence, healthier relationships and greater life satisfaction. Contrariwise, excessive patterns of avoidance lead to opposite outcomes.

The critical significance of facing situations involving psychological pain helps us introduce an overlapping and key concept, acceptance. As will become clear throughout this book, we cannot untangle avoidance from acceptance. Fundamentally, we need to accept the realities of facing and enduring, as well as the negative outcomes that occur with excessive avoidance of such. A main theme of this book is that avoidance is the predominant cause and/or maintenance factor of most chronic psychological problems, including depression. Examples of this theme are seen in post-traumatic stress patients who do not want to discuss their dramatic experiences, drug/alcohol abusers who suppress their awareness of negative memories with psychoactive substances and other escape behaviors, eating disorder patients who displace their control issues with inappropriate and distracting food intake, gamblers who escape from their internal conflicts with compulsive acts, sexual compulsives who run away from intimacy and vulnerability, dependent personalities who continue to be indecisive and over rely on others, and people who escape into the world of the internet. The examples (contents) are almost endless but the themes (processes) are characteristically the same. That is, avoidance of some combination of thoughts, feelings and behaviors, along with associated lack of acceptance, combine as core issues which drive psychological disorders such as chronic depression. With respect to treatment, there will be clear articulations of how we can overcome persistent avoidance and lack of acceptance in the chapters to come.

What form does the lack of acceptance typically take? Generally, individuals engage in excessive lack of acceptance with respect to one or more of three aspects: themselves (Self), how they view and react to people (Others), and how they perceive living (Life). Certainly, it is expected that all of us will have trouble accepting some experiences. We hear about atrocities, learn a loved one has died, have relationship problems, etc. Clearly, it is natural to experience denial and/or a difficulty accepting stressful life experiences. Often, it takes a great deal of time and psychological work to truly accept traumatic realities at an emotional level. Most of us, most of the time, eventually come to accept the reality of our experiences and move on with our life in constructive ways and with more maturity. However, this process can be delayed significantly or indefinitely via inappropriate patterns of avoidance and lack of acceptance. In extreme cases we can become mired in dysfunctional patterns leading to chronic depression and cycles of self-defeating behavior. As implied above, this book will demonstrate how avoidance and acceptance issues are instrumental in causing and sustaining most psychological problems. Whereas the bulk of material will focus on chronic depression, the underlying themes of causation outlined in this book can be applied to many other common psychological disorders, such as those involving anxiety, personality, and substance abuse disorders which often co-occur in various combinations due to their shared core issues. Thus, although this book will concentrate on how depression tends to be caused and/or sustained, the underlying processes and causations discussed are relevant for many other disorders that can occur independently or in combination with depression.

Chapter Two

Avoiders

The relevance of approach and avoidances forces in our daily lives was introduced in Chapter One. In Chapter Two we will expand on this topic and introduce associated research data. Dollard & Miller (1950) performed groundbreaking work on the relationship between avoidance and approach forces in terms of their effects on motivation and behavior decades ago. Briefly, they reasoned that the relative strength of these forces helps determine whether we approach or avoid goal directed outcomes. More specifically, they found that when motivation to approach a goal is stronger than the motivation to avoid it, then action towards achieving the goal prevails. They not only demonstrated these relationships in experiments but also found that, as we get closer to obtaining a goal, avoidance forces (anxiety and fear) go up at a faster rate than approach forces (desire). Moreover, when avoidance forces are stronger than approach ones it is predicted that the organism will discontinue goal directed activity.

For example, let's say that John wants to ask out a gal for a date next Saturday night. The Monday before he is likely to experience a great deal of positive anticipation but little anxiety because it is still a few days away from when he planned to pop the question. At this point in time, his approach forces are likely greater than his avoidance ones. He can imagine the fun and activities with which they could participate. However, as the time approaches for him to ask her out, the intensity of his feelings of avoidance are predicted to rise more steeply than approach ones. If his anxiety grows stronger than his desire before his asks her out, then he will almost assuredly engage in avoidant behavior and may even justify it (i.e., come up with some rationalization or excuse) in order to protect his self-esteem. In this type of situation, his avoidant behavior is under the principle of negative reinforcement because his avoidance of asking her out is followed with relief of anxiety or fear. Note that anxiety involves imaginary contact whereas fear involves the presence of the actual person or object. In this type of case his avoidant behavior is negatively reinforced (i.e., strengthened by the consequences that follow it); that is, relief from anxiety or fear. Since negative reinforcement, like positive reinforcement, is expected to increase response probability in similar situations, it is predicted that henceforth he will display avoidant behavior in like situations. This type of analysis helps explain why people with specific phobias and panic disorder, untreated or treated unsuccessfully, can develop more generalized conditions such as agoraphobia. Note also that because we evaluate our behavioral patterns, avoidant behaviors can have important implications for our self-concept. Thus, when people consistently avoid various stressors, responsibilities and desired outcomes, they can easily develop the self-perception of being weak or a coward. Once this type of self-concept orientation develops, it can mediate a whole host of related behaviors. In other words, it can generalize to other situations involving approach vs. avoidance forces wherein individuals are quick to run away without even evaluating their choices, since they perceive themselves as incapable of approaching certain stimuli. After all, they may think; "I can't do this because I lack the intestinal fortitude." In essence, some people come to see themselves as Avoiders. Of course, this can be a long and winding road toward self-defeat and one that, at least initially, they did not envision as landing them in a state of depression.

These opposing forces are inescapable parts of our evolution. They are designed for survival as opposed to helping make us happier and/or more content, although certain stimuli and responses naturally give us pleasure in the short run. Given that we are vulnerable to a multitude of factors that can lead to our demise, it is crucial we are careful to avoid certain stimuli and circumstances which can be dangerous. At the same time however, we are sometimes required to take risks and face painful situations in order to survive. We may need to consent to cardiac surgery or fight off someone who attacks us. Although the dividing line between prudent decisions to face versus avoid situations is not always clear, it is proposed here that people with chronic depression tend to habitually engage in avoidance of situations that either leads to self-defeating effects and/or lack of personal growth. Certainly, there are times when it is wise to avoid situations that will only cause us to waste energy and resources or risk serious injury or death. On the other hand, it is imperative we confront situations consistent with our values and priorities, particularly when we may not get another opportunity to do so or are simply putting off the inevitable (i.e., will have to face the stressful situation at some later date anyway), and delaying action only makes matters worse.

Contemporary research has found physiological support for Dollard and Miller's analyses via physiological mapping of our brains (Rogers, 2004). For example, in recent years research has not only made us more aware of the positive aspects of anger but, at the same time, located specific brain centers for approach vs. avoidance motivation with respect to these emotions. It seems surprising that it has taken us so long to be aware of the advantages of anger, given the assumption that it must have some evolutionary utility. Most likely, our view of anger is biased by the radical actions that some engage in when enraged, as well as the physiological and cognitive distress sometimes associated with this emotion. Nevertheless, research is revealing that anger can fuel optimism, foster leadership, increase focus on the practical issues, heighten creativity and ambition, enhance emotional intelligence, and facilitate understanding of others. As for the physiological bases of approach and avoidance, brain imaging and electrical studies have shown that the left frontal lobe is involved with approach behaviors toward desired goals and is rewarding in logical and rational ways. Avoidance behaviors are associated with activation of the right frontal cortex and entwined with a negative motivational system affiliated with inhibition and escape from punishment and threat. Brain scans reveal that anger leads to significant activation of the left anterior cortex, thereby facilitating positive approach behaviors. Thus, this area of research not only demonstrates physiological foundations for Dollard and Miller's concepts of approach and avoidance but, at the same time, provides evidence that anger can be a pleasurable experience when we believe it can help facilitate positive changes.

Consistent with this type of finding, we are moving away from the perspective that emotions are either positive or negative. Instead, emotions are now being viewed as providing "motivational direction," whereby they either stimulate approach or avoidance/withdrawal behaviors. Generally speaking, when we get angry we have a biologically rooted tendency to get connected with what made us feel this way and to try to get rid of it. Nevertheless, whether anger is positive or negative in effects largely depends on the situation and whether or not we have constructive options. Nevertheless, the data available suggest that we should not work too hard to suppress it. Typically, it is better to let anger unfold (i.e., accept it as temporary and natural) rather than try to suppress or control it.

Obviously, how and when we approach and avoid certain stimuli show a great deal of individual variation. What accounts for these differences? Presumably, our learning history is primarily responsible for these individual differences. Behaviors followed by pleasant circumstances tend to become more likely over time whereas behaviors followed by unpleasant experiences have a penchant to decrease in probability. As a result, we all avoid some situations and approach others and the combination of these is unique to each person. Nevertheless, as you traverse through the ensuing chapters, it is expected that you will be struck by the pervasive power of avoidance factors associated with social interactions and relationships. Accordingly, chronic depression generally involves some type of avoidance of others. This should not be too surprising if we keep in mind we are "Social Animals" (Aronson, 2013). According to Aronson, we can't escape our mammalian roots which are inherently social. Consequently, we need love, recognition, approval, attention, etc. from others whether we admit it or not. On the other hand, particular people are usually associated with our most painful life experiences. The inherent nature of our social selves is evident even when we are alone or asleep and can't help but think about others in our imagination and dreams. Just try not to think about others on an occasion when you're alone. It is difficult for most people to go even a few minutes without some type of people-oriented thoughts. As a result of the dominance of our social needs, our motivational conflicts frequently center on issues involving rejection, love, loneliness, embarrassment, disapproval, dependency, jealousy, anger, guilt, etc. It is situations and reactions involving these types of emotional conflicts that are so often at the epicenter of the psychological paralysis and habitual avoidance of the depressed individual. Without question, the most common presenting problems brought to this author in psychotherapy have revolved around social interaction and relationship issues. Of course, there is little that can be done about the way we are biologically wired (hardware). However, there is much that can be learned and changed in terms of our choices and the consequences that accrue as a result (software), which is the focus of this book.

Relevant Research by Author

From 1997 through 2009, the principal author administered the same psychological screening test to over 1200 psychotherapy outpatients. These outpatients were engaged in individual or marital counseling, so follow-up clinical observations on the validity of their test results in terms of diagnoses could be qualitatively assessed. The test utilized, the Millon Clinical Multiaxial Inventory-III (MCMI-III), allows for assessment of clinical syndromes such as anxiety, depression, drug and alcohol abuse and thought disorder, as well as most forms of personality disorder. Over the many years that the MCMI-III was administered to these outpatients, this author witnessed certain trends in terms of what kinds of personalities were associated with chronic depression. The same kinds of personality patterns were appearing repeatedly. After many years of seeing these trends, a decision was made to put this enormous amount of data in a computer and see what it would spit out. The hypothesis, not surprisingly, was that personality traits and disorders associated predominately with avoidant coping styles would show a much higher correlation with chronic depression than personalities not characterized by such. The findings are particularly relevant to the discussion of avoidance patterns and how they can cause and sustain depression (Church, Kohlert & Brooks, 2013). Interestingly, it was found that individuals who scored significantly on the Dysthymia Scale, a measure of chronic depression, displayed their most frequent and significant elevations on the following personality patterns scales: Depressive (pessimistic/cynical), Dependent (submissive), Masochistic (self-sacrificing), Negativistic (passive-aggressive), and Avoidant (hypersensitive). Note also that the percentages of significantly elevated Dysthymia scorers were 69%, 64%, 50%, 50%, and 48%, respectively for these personality scales. What are we to make of the very high percentages and statistically significant correlations found with this large sample? Although these findings may be surprising to some, they are in line with the clinical feedback and impressions obtained by this author with these and many other outpatients, many of whom were in psychotherapy for well over a year. That is, people with chronic depression reveal patterns of avoidance and/or escape from internal and/or external stressors which, in most cases, helped cause and/or sustain their depression and/or other psychological and practical life problems. Of course, it is also possible that in some cases depression facilitated avoidance and escape patterns. Whatever the case, the client is often caught in a vicious cycle that is very difficult to exit. Their personality styles tend to cause them to become and stay depressed while their state of depression robs them of the energy, motivation and positive attitudes prerequisite to engaging in less avoidance and escape behaviors. Note that similar findings were reported for Major Depression, PTSD and Anxiety. As for Major Depression, it should be mentioned that this disorder is very often recurrent and sometimes chronic in nature. At any rate, the same personality patterns associated with causing and sustaining Dysthymia were suggested with Major Depression, PTSD and Anxiety Disorders.

While pondering the meaning of these results, it became intuitively obvious that there is a basic theme cutting through the personalities of most individuals suffering from chronic depression. Put another way, the research data were congruent with what the author found in clinical work with his clients; that is, chronic patterns of avoidance are strongly correlated with depression and related psychological disorders. This constellation of personality characteristics, reflecting consistent and significant patterns of avoidance and escape behaviors, thoughts and feelings, are coined Avoiders for the purposes of this book. Avoider refers to people who utilize avoidance and escape patterns excessively and inappropriately, such that these patterns significantly reduce their psychological functioning. What follows below is discussion of how distinct avoidant patterns of personality were related to chronic depression in the MCMI study. However, it should be noted that these personality patterns correlate highly (i.e., they overlap a great deal). Thus, people high on the Dependent Scale tend to be high on the Masochism Scale and those high on Avoidant tend to be high on Depressive and vice versa.

In essence, the Depressive style reflects relatively pessimistic, cynical and skeptical thought processes. These individuals avoid thinking positively so as to not be too disappointed or upset when things don't go well. They protect themselves from falling too far from rejection, failure, and other negative experiences. In other words, they desperately guard against getting disappointed, demoralized or depressed. Of course, this means they often create unexpected negative outcomes with self-fulfilling prophecies and the reduction of experiencing pleasure.

The Dependent style reveals tendencies toward avoiding decisions, responsibilities and possible abandonment by others. They avoid developing a full sense of identity and tend to "piggyback" on others, even when they possess the requisite competence to adapt well. Because they often allow their fate to be determined by others, they have a penchant to externalize blame when things don't go well. This allows them to avoid or escape from feelings of inadequacy that would otherwise cause them psychological pain in the short term.

The Avoidant style involves tendencies toward being hypersensitive to rejection, embarrassment, disapproval, criticism and interpersonal conflict. Consequently, individuals high on this scale tend to avoid situations that could lead to negative thoughts or feelings from social interactions.

The Masochistic style revolves around propensities toward being self-sacrificing, self-effacing and deferent. These people have a tendency to let others get their way by subjugating their wants and needs. They are people pleasers who avoid full development of their identities. Not unexpectedly, they tend to be taken for granted and advantage of which, of course, helps ferment resentment and frustration into anger which can ultimately transform into feelings of sadness and helplessness.

The Negativistic style avoids assertive communication of wants and needs. These individuals tend to vacillate between being passive versus aggressive with both verbal and non-verbal communication. Obviously, these patterns tend to alienate others, create and maintain low self-esteem, and cause underachievement in numerous areas of functioning.

Basically, Avoiders go through life experiencing pervasive anxiety and fear. They find it very difficult to be satisfied or content on a regular basis. When their security needs are being met, their anxieties and fears tend to be low and they appear to function rather normally. However, they cannot escape the reality of being an underachiever in many domains which, at minimum, plagues them with underlying discontent, vague feelings of regret or shame, frustrations, unfinished business and unmet life goals. Generally, they have difficulty in expressing their wants and feelings in mature ways, thereby causing negative emotions to be bottled up. This diminishes the likelihood they will be treated respectfully while increasing the probability they will overreact emotionally at times by knocking a nail in with a sledge hammer when a regular hammer would have sufficed.

The Relationship between Avoidance and Acceptance (The Case of Ramona)

The Case Study of Ramona provides an excellent example and introduction to the inextricable relationship between avoidance and acceptance. Her case was short-term and not particularly complicated. We will return to discussion of the relevance of her case in a subsequent section (Case Studies) of the book. For now, we will focus on how avoidance and acceptance processes were intertwined in her life.

A car accident left Ramona with significantly less capacity to do physical things, along with pain and discomfort on a regular basis, despite taking numerous medications for relief. For the first time in her life, this middle-aged mom could not engage fully in activities she considered normal. She was particularly upset that she could no longer play physically with her children in ways they were accustomed. What drove her into therapy was the observation that she was particularly moody and irritable with her husband and the kids. She let her frustrations and anger be displaced on the people who meant the most to her and felt terrible about it. She was confused and didn't know what to do. Also, she had become reclusive and typically didn't want to do anything with anyone, including activities she once enjoyed and could still perform. She was pushing people away with her anger and attitudes, reflected in the following statement: "If I can't do things the way I used to, then I don't want to do anything." Essentially, she was depressed and felt sorry for herself. It was clear that she hadn't accepted significant life alterations associated with the accident. This was preventing her from adapting constructively to her new circumstances. As long as she avoided the reality of her limitations and chronic pain post-accident, she could not move forward in positive ways. Eventually she was guided into seeing how her avoidant patterns were impeding acceptance of her "new life" and adjustments associated with it. Once she faced her pain and her lessened capabilities, she was able to move forward with acceptance which meant living her life according to her primary value (family-orientated) system.

We will return to her case in Chapter Five. Her case was presented here to accent the point that people with chronic depression usually need to become aware that non-acceptance of their condition is grounded in excessive patterns of avoidance. Further, they often do not know what needs to be accepted until they stop avoiding so much. For example, the author recalls an obese woman who didn't realize her avoidance of weight loss was driven by her discomfort with being treated like a sexual object by her husband and other men; or a man who engaged in masturbation to pornography to avoid his fears of having intercourse with women; and numerous kleptomaniacs who stole things they didn't really want or need to temporarily escape from painful life circumstances. How can we truly get at the bottom line with our self-defeating behaviors and chronic mood issues if we do not know what we are avoiding?

Chapter Three

Chronic Depression

It is extremely common to hear the word depression come up in everyday conversation. People mention how sad they get during winter, how depressing the news has been lately, discuss how someone they know suffers from depression, and talk about the newest antidepressant medication. At the same time, the superficiality of these conversations may seem striking, as they often gloss over distinctions between different types of depression, as well as their varied etiologies and treatments. It is as though depression is seen as an inevitable condition that we must endure until treated in some straightforward and simplistic fashion. It is spoken of as if it is commonplace and contagious, like the flu or a cold that will simply go away or respond to some form of simple and direct treatment.

With regard antidepressant medication, billions of dollars per year is spent on creating, producing, selling, distributing, advertising, marketing and prescribing such. Surprisingly, most prescriptions (estimated at 80%) are managed by non-psychiatric medical practitioners for people with psychological and/or substance abuse problems (Levant, 2002). This prompts us to ask whether this type of medical model treatment is much different than utilizing medications for high blood pressure or thyroid dysfunction. At least these conditions have more rational bases for diagnosis and logical ways of detecting whether treatment is having a discernible effect. A more in-depth look at the medical model approach to treatment of depression prompts several important questions. For example, do antidepressants treat much more than symptoms? How often do antidepressant medications and the assumptions underlying their use distract people from looking at and addressing the core causes of their depression? What are the potential side effects of antidepressant medication, and do some people avoid psychotherapy because they do not want to do the hard work necessary to overcome the core causes of depression?

There are many different forms of depression and people are much more aware of some types than others. Most people have at least some limited knowledge of Bipolar and Major Depression Disorders, as they receive a fair amount of notoriety. Oppositely, chronic depression (formerly Dysthymia and currently referred to as Persistent Depressive Disorder) have received sparse attention and, surprisingly, the author has found that most outpatient clients and psychiatrically hospitalized patients have never heard of Dysthymia or Persistent Depressive Disorder.

It is not clear why most people are so unaware of the frequency and nature of chronic depression. Perhaps, it is because the chronic form tends to be more subtle in effects (symptoms). People with bipolar and major depressive conditions tend to display symptoms that are much more overt and severe. Their behaviors and the consequences surrounding them are generally far more dramatic, extreme and vivid than those with chronic depression. Suicide attempts, psychiatric hospitalization and medication utilization are much more common with Major Depression and Bipolar Disorder than chronic depression (Dysthymia or Persistent Depressive Disorder).

The relative lack of knowledge of chronic depression is quite surprising when we consider that it is estimated that it afflicts between 3 to 5% of the population (Sue, et. al., 2013). This suggests that somewhere between ten to fifteen million people suffer from chronic depression in the United States. However, we need to consider that this estimate may seriously underestimate the number of people with this condition. Along these lines, people suffering from chronic depression tend to be "silent sufferers" who fly under the radar. Typically they continue to work, go to school, care for their families and seem to the casual observer to function in the normal range. Most learn to tolerate their depressive state and many don't even know they suffer from this form of psychological disorder. Their condition often begins early in life and sufferers often labor with depression for a very long time before they realize what they have been enduring. Eventually, they become aware that most people enjoy life more than they do, and that their chronic state of discontent has become a way of life; a kind of developmental depression that has grown insidiously, settling into the fiber of their being. Some practitioners do not take their mild to moderate symptoms seriously because, relative to people suffering from Bipolar and Major Depression, they seem miniscule. However, irrespective of degree, suffering continuously from anything is quite difficult for most people. How would you like to have long-term and continuous pain and discomfort from a headache, cold, allergy, arthritis, etc. that vacillates from mild to moderate in intensity? Does it seem so minor when you think of it in this way?

The American Psychiatric Association's Diagnostic and Statistical Manual-V (2013) defines chronic depression or, persistent depressive disorder (PDD), as consisting of depressive symptoms: "Most of the day and for more days than not during a two-year period." Symptoms include pessimism or guilt, loss of interest, or appetite or overeating, low self-esteem, chronic fatigue, social withdrawal, and concentration difficulties.

The prevalence for PDD is greater for women than men. Theoretical explanations for PDD include many causative factors, such as: repressed anger following significant relationship loss, lack or lower availability of rewarding events in one's life, poor social skills, negative and distorted beliefs and perspectives, a pattern of "learned helplessness" created by environmental influences, a ruminative style of dwelling on the negative, overwhelming amounts of stress, socio-cultural factors and adaptations, and significant medical conditions (Sue, Sue & Sue, 2013).

Upon review of the above stated causative factors of depression, is it surprising that antidepressant medication has been found to be relatively ineffective with chronic depression while often effective with Major Depression and Bipolar Disorder (Szalavitz, 2010)? Meta-analyses, which involve combining the results of scores of research studies into a single statistical analysis, have revealed this distinction. That is, patients with chronic mild to moderate range depression improve at about the same frequency as individuals in placebo groups (about one-third of the time). So, they appear to benefit little from the antidepressant medication apart from expectancy effects. Patients with Major Depression and Bipolar

Disorder show overall improvement rates with antidepressant medication significantly above the "placebo effect."

As the reader will see, these findings are consonant with the notion that chronic depression is primarily related to avoidance patterns. Thus, there is little reason to believe that antidepressant medication should have much benefit with Avoiders, except perhaps in the early stages of helping them "get over the hump" in terms of facing the needed changes in their perspectives and coping styles. Of course, much of the improvement in the initial stages may be due to expectancy (placebo) effects. As for Major depression, significant stressors are thought to disrupt neurotransmitter functioning. The prevailing thought is that antidepressant medication, in ways we do not entirely understand, helps with the influence of key neurotransmitters, more specifically, serotonin, norepinephrine and/or dopamine. However, it should be pointed out that our scientific understanding at this point is so unsophisticated that the choice of which antidepressant medications to use is essentially trial and error. The truth is that there is no way to precisely know whether a neurotransmitter problem actually exists, how it will affect mood, which medication would be most beneficial (if any), and what dosage is most appropriate. Therefore, medications are utilized in a hypothetical (educated guess) manner with the subjective responses of the patient the major determinant of which medication(s) are prescribed, how much, and for how long. With regard to Bipolar Disorder, research is clear in establishing a biological basis as pre-dispositional in nature. As a result, it is believed that mood stabilizing medication can play a significant role in helping these patients with depression. Nevertheless, the greater impact with medication for patients suffering from Major Depression and Bipolar Disorders does not mean these sufferers may not also display avoidant and escape patterns (i.e., be Avoiders). In these cases, avoidant patterns could also play a cause and/or effect role on depression. We must remember that co-morbidity rates run very high. It has been estimated that as many as 75% of people with one psychological disorder have two or more (Sue, et. al., 2013). Thus, it is anticipated that many people with significant psychological disorders such as Major Depression and Bipolar Disorder have concurrent personality, anxiety, drug/alcohol and/or other disorders that are associated with avoidance and escape patterns that, at the very least, help maintain and exacerbate depression symptoms.

Chapter Four

Roads to Depression and Treatment Options

This chapter discusses various treatment options for depression with an emphasis upon specific orientations developed by this author. As it will be seen, it is the author's contention that all formal psychotherapies, as well as lay approaches such as those utilized by Alcoholics Anonymous, are effective to some extent because they help individuals confront and work through issues of avoidance, acceptance and purposeful activity. As will be discussed, purposeful activity is also related to acceptance because humans need to be guided by goals derived from their values. If we do not accept this fundamental aspect of life, we almost certainly will fall prey to chronic depression and an aimless existence. The degree to which issues of avoidance, acceptance and purpose need to be addressed will, of course, vary with life circumstances, maturity level, personality style and a variety of other variables. More specifically, some people will be experiencing significant difficulties with patterns of avoidance whereas others may be struggling with key issues of acceptance or minimal purposes for living. Still others will be struggling with some combination of two or all three of these fundamental aspects of life. As a result, the focus of therapeutic encounters will vary a good deal and could even change over time within an individual. With respect to the latter, some people may need to focus on what they are not accepting or lack of purpose before they can confront what they have been avoiding. On the other hand, others may need to confront what they have been avoiding before they can develop greater insight into what they haven't been accepting and/or create more meaningful goals or greater focus and commitment to such. Before covering these concepts in actual case studies in the next chapter, a brief review of some basic tenets of Acceptance and Commitment (ACT) will be discussed because this therapeutic model is closely aligned with the main themes of this book. Subsequently, more traditional models of therapy will be covered in order to show how they also overlap with the concept of Avoiders and can be applied in the process of helping people engage in constructive change.

The Eclectic Approach of ACT

Acceptance and Commitment Therapy (ACT), a very contemporary approach, is considered an advanced form of cognitive behavioral therapy (Hayes, et. al, 2010). It is comprised of a blend of theoretical models, including the traditional cognitive-behavioral therapy (CBT). The ACT approach is particularly well-suited to cases that are more emotion than problem/solution focused (i.e., acceptance based). Anyone who has treated a broad spectrum of adults with psychological problems is aware that many, if not most, of the primary issues dealt with in psychotherapy are emotion focused. In other words, ones in which the client needs to accept the limitations of what they can actually change, along with the inevitable and natural pain associated with stress, loss, medical problems that cannot be remedied, etc. Thus, their "psychological disorder" is often a natural reaction to their life situation which is mainly the result of circumstances they have backed themselves into (internal causation). ACT tends to help move clients away from trying to control their feelings and thoughts and toward acceptance of the relatively transient and situational states of emotional pain. At the same time, clients are guided toward enhanced commitment to purposeful living. On the contrary, traditional cognitive behavioral methods tend to look for a solution or remedy for psychological problems. Of course, this is sometimes a very constructive and appropriate way to look at the client's situation. Therefore, it will be very important from the start of therapy for the client and counselor to determine whether a solution/problem focused type of treatment or acceptance/emotion based approach or both is most suitable. More specifically, ACT focuses on six processes, namely: a) contact with the present moment, b) acceptance, c) defusion (not letting oneself be defined by self-evaluative labels or constructs which are stereotypic attributions of a negative nature); e.g., "I act this way because I'm a sick depressed person," d) self as context, e) values and f) committed action. As the reader will see, the author collapses these six processes into three domains, namely: Avoidance, Acceptance and Purposeful Activity when utilizing an ACT type of approach with clients. Conceptually, defusion and self as context are seen as parts of Acceptance whereas values and committed action are integrated into Purposeful Activity. Avoidance is viewed as a separate component because of its vital importance. An important way this book differs from a pure ACT approach is that traditional methods of psychotherapy are retained because many of their methods are beneficial (e.g. assertiveness training, rational thinking, relaxation methods, values clarification).

Prior to discussing treatment in greater detail, key terms and conceptual categories will be presented so the reader will have a framework with which to understand what is being proposed. This book also differs from ACT by utilizing a more traditional definition of avoidance and the creation of categorizations for various types of avoiders and acceptance barriers. Moreover, succinct and straightforward treatment goals for avoidance and acceptance limitations are advanced.

Avoidance

Avoidance is defined as the act of terminating or escaping from unpleasant emotions, thoughts or actions. Essentially, this definition is consistent with negative reinforcement, a term associated with operant conditioning (Watson, 2007). This well-documented principle of operant conditioning has revealed that avoidance or escape from an aversive circumstance or object is rewarded (reinforced) by the relief associated with terminating unpleasantness associated with it. Thus, avoidant behavior is more likely to occur in the future because learning has occurred; i.e., reinforcement via feelings of relief. Technically speaking, avoidance and escape are separate aspects of negative reinforcement since the former involves circumventing unpleasantness while the latter ends the aversive experience. For purposes of this book, the terms avoidance and escape are used loosely and interchangeably. For the most part, the term avoidance will be used for simplicity/brevity sake. At any rate, the most important thing to remember is both fall under the rubric of negative reinforcement and, as will be pointed out repeatedly, are crucial factors to consider with respect to understanding and treating Avoiders.

Avoiders

Five basic types of Avoiders are delineated in this book and described below. Note that these are not mutually exclusive types, as they overlap to some degree and can co-occur (i.e., a person can fit into more than one category type). Nevertheless, they will be described independently because most people have a dominant type of avoidance pattern (i.e., can be characterized best by one of the five types).

A) **Runners** - The Runner consistently avoids negative emotions and stressful situations, particularly those involving anxiety and fear, in order to obtain relief from these unpleasant states.

B) **Denier** - The Denier characteristically refuses to confront and accept reality while being prone to wishful thinking and refusal to admit to problems, weaknesses or inadequacies.

C) **Blamer** - The Blamer reveals a strong penchant toward attributing negative circumstances and events to other people and situational factors, thereby protecting their self-esteem.

D) **Irresponsible** - The Irresponsible displays the propensity to fail to follow through with expected and appropriate duties, responsibilities and obligations, thereby dumping them on the shoulders of others.

E) **Escape Artist** - Escape artists engage in excessive egocentric and self-defeating thoughts and behaviors in order to distract themselves from uncomfortable and distressing realities and situations.

Treatment Goals for Reducing Avoidance Patterns

1) Discuss the role of avoidance in the causation and/or maintenance of depression.

2) Help the client see how avoidance is related to their depression.

3) De-emphasize the notion that depression is "the problem" while helping the client to see that depression is a side effect of avoidance patterns and/or situational factors.

4) Assist the client in identification of persons and/or situations that reinforce and enable their avoidance patterns and thereby help maintain their depression.

5) Stress that their anxieties and fears, like other aspects of suffering, are inevitable and natural parts of the human condition but do not have to prevent them from living their life fully and meaningfully.

6) Explain that avoidance patterns are habitual and, as a result, will require a good deal of patience and motivated effort to change and overcome.

7) Describe the proposed treatment plan (traditional and/or ACT-type) so they can have a choice to agree, disagree or amend the goals and methods utilized, as well as clarify the rationale for such.

Acceptance

Acceptance is defined as the relatively accurate awareness and genuine acknowledgment of our past, present and future realities. It should be mentioned here that acceptance is not quitting or an "I must give up" attitude. The concept of Acceptance does not imply that nothing can be done about a given situation or psychological state at hand. Rather, it involves a very frank and realistic look at life circumstances, limitations and alternatives.

As previously discussed, we can potentially have difficulty with

Acceptance in one or more of three domains: Self, Others and Life. Further, each domain is broken down into seven specific categories where difficulty can occur (see below). Note then that a given individual may demonstrate one or more types of problems with acceptance in one or more domains.

Self	Others	Life
Entitled	Alienating	Helpless
Grandiose	Controlling	Noncreative
Hypersensitive	Distrustful	Nonreciprocal
Perfectionistic	Impractical	Pessimistic
Self-Centered	Naive	Meaningless
Self-Debasing	Reactive	Rigid
Unforgiving	Unemotional	Simplistic

Acceptance of Self

With respect to self-orientation, the Entitled can be characterized as possessive, self-centered, insecure and lacking in empathy. The Grandiose can be described as having over-inflated views of their abilities, as well as unrealistic expectations and goals. The Hypersensitive over-personalizes and over-reacts to disapproval, rejection and criticism. Perfectionists have pronounced difficulty accepting mistakes, failures and imperfections. The Self-Centered are almost exclusively focused on self and, therefore, neither care about nor understand others well. The Self-Debasing person is self-critical and has trouble accepting who they are. They are their own worst critic. Unforgiving people hold grudges toward themselves while perceiving they do not deserve happiness and may even feel they should be punished by others and/or themselves.

Acceptance of Others

Alienating individuals are passive-aggressive, rejecting, angry and unforgiving toward others. The Controller is dogmatic, dominating and manipulative. The Distrustful can be typified as suspicious, cautious and hyper-vigilant. The Impractical can be described as wishful in thinking, prone to see the world in black versus white terms and unrealistic in their expectations of others' actions and reactions. Naïve individuals can be characterized as Pollyanna-like and overly trusting. The Reactive tends to be loud, spontaneous, impulsive and overly emotional. Unemotional types are withdrawn, cold and unaffectionate.

Acceptance of Life

The Helpless tend to think they will get by or get what they want via external locus of control (i.e., dependent on others, luck, fate or intervention by powerful forces). The Meaningless go through sustained periods without experiencing sufficient purpose from a set of self-derived values and goals. The Noncreative lives according to thinking "inside the box" while failing to find their own creative answers while adjusting to changes in themselves, as well as the wicked curves that life can throw at us. The Nonreciprocal does not accept that most of the time we get what we deserve while not seeing that they have been acting in ways that should realistically be expected to yield little. Although they frequently complain that life isn't fair, they are in fact getting pretty much what they have earned. Pessimists hold onto cynical and negative life views whether or not any evidence supports their positions. The Rigid are essentially set in stone with inflexible and immutable thinking and actions (or lack thereof). The Simplistic person refuses to see the "big picture" or "gray areas" of life while being content to live day-to-day without much introspection or reflection.

Treatment Goals for Building Acceptance

Although more specific examples and methods for increasing acceptance will be presented in the next chapter on Case Studies, the basic steps are outlined below.

1) Increase awareness of the role of acceptance in causing and/or sustaining depression.

2) Explain that acceptance is neither a process of giving up nor a fix. Rather, it is an attitude of openness and an effort to be as realistic as possible about oneself, others and life in general.

3) Discuss how lack of acceptance is related to avoidance and how both interact and help cause and maintain depression.

4) Assess the types of Self, Other and Life Acceptance difficulties the client possesses and engage him/her in examination of how these have caused and/or sustained their depression, including how they may have defined themselves as a depressed person, thereby making it more difficult to imagine a better life and effectuate change.

5) Identify whether significant others or life situations are inhibiting or blocking acceptance of important realities and/or reinforcing patterns of avoidance, such as dependent, irresponsible and immature behaviors.

6) Emphasize how it is easier to engage in Acceptance when we have strong value-driven purposes which add meaning to life, help us confront stress, and motivate constructive and positive goal directed behaviors.

7) Discuss how acceptance can be increased via realistic self-talk. In Chapter Seven there is presentation of the principal author's list of key acceptance related perspectives that can be used effectively for this purpose.

Purposeful Actions

Purpose towards a meaningful life cannot be underestimated in terms of its importance in relation to avoidance and acceptance processes. Without a strong sense of purpose and associated actions, it is extremely difficult to overcome avoidance forces and accept difficult realities. Moreover, a strong capacity to overcome avoidance and acceptance issues will be difficult when we lack strong commitment toward purposeful goals. The bottom line is that a life without meaning is a meaningless and aimless existence.

Purpose derives from a coherent and clear set of life values that develop and strengthen over time. It is through commitment to a core set of values that we derive a sense of meaning and purpose in life. Purposeful action refers to behaviors that we perform consistent with our values. Clearly, our purposes will make little difference if we do little more than give lip service to them. To put it bluntly, a strong set of purposeful activities, backed up by behavioral follow through, help keep us from getting buried in an avalanche of life stressors. These pillars give us the strength to withstand enormous waves of conflict, stress and confusion.

Inhibitions of Purposeful Activity

There are a number of ways that we can get into trouble in this important life area, especially because most of us are living longer than previous generations, and changes in society are occurring much more rapidly. Thus, we find ourselves having to modify and clarify our values and goals as we move through many developmental and situational changes, both expected and unexpected. The most common difficulties revealed by people in terms of purposeful activity are shown below.

1) **Lack of sufficient purpose in life** - In this case, individuals may have some minimal purpose but clearly not enough to motivate them toward constructive goals on a regular basis.

2) **Vague purposes which lack clarity and refinement** - In this situation persons can state they would like to be happier, feel at peace, be more productive or creative but cannot specify what would have to change in order for them to reach these goals. For example, do they feel that they are in a job rather than a career or married only in a nominal sense? If so, what would they have to do to get to a better place? Do they have to go back to school, look for a different job or engage in marital enrichment or counseling?

3) **Behavioral action consistent with purposes and values is inhibited** - Sometimes we know what is important but have difficulty in following through with purposeful action. This can occur because of vague or conflicting values, lack of knowledge as to how to accomplish our goal, lack of energy, distraction by other competing issues in our life, or a defensive response set (e.g.,

"I have time to make these changes, they don't have to be done right away").

Treatment Goals for Purposeful Actions

A) The integral role of purposeful action is discussed.

B) Assessment of purposeful motivation and commitment are accomplished, along with evaluation of important life values and goals.

C) Feedback is given to the client in terms of whether their current sets of values and purposes are well defined or not, and whether they appear essential enough to give them a sense of meaning and the strength to overcome avoidance forces and acceptance limitations. Also, assessment of whether or not their goals are realistic and appropriate is accomplished.

D) If required, the client is challenged to creatively develop and/or extend life purposes congruent with their values.

E) If needed, values clarification and goal modification are undertaken.

F) Discussion of the crucial nature of purposeful action in line with their goals ensues, along with specific actions consistent with them, is undertaken.

Traditional Treatment Methods

Often, traditional treatment methods are sufficient in helping individuals get over chronic depression. However, it should be emphasized that traditional methods tend to be less comprehensive and more superficial in treatment than ACT type approaches. Nevertheless, most would agree that we don't need to do surgery when less invasive methods will do the trick. In other words if traditional methods are insufficient, then more intensive methods can be utilized subsequently or utilized concurrently.

Over the last several decades, a variety of traditional approaches have been shown to be effective in ameliorating depression and other psychological disorders. As pointed out earlier, it is this author's opinion that the success of these therapies is largely the result of their aiding clients in reducing avoidance, and/or increasing acceptance and purposeful action. These methods can be used independently or in conjunction with the ACT-type model proposed in this book. A concise look at common traditional therapeutic methodologies is presented below.

Behavior Therapies

Behavior therapy presumes that avoidance is essentially learned due to the power of negative reinforcement. That is, we learn to avoid and escape unpleasantness or pain even though this coping style may not be in our long-term best interest. Consistent with this notion, we can learn to engage in avoidance less and more appropriately. Fortunately, a variety of therapeutic interventions have been designed to help extinguish avoidant and escape behaviors.

Systematic desensitization, spearheaded by Wolpe (1958), involves getting patients into a relaxed state and then directing them to visualize successfully approaching and engaging in situations they fear from a graduated hierarchy (i.e., least to most feared). They are asked to hold onto their visualizations until relaxation essentially wins out over their anxiety related to the scenes they are imagining. The conceptual framework here is that one cannot be anxious and relaxed at the same time. Eventually, the anxious response will be nullified by relaxation allowing the individual to overcome their inhibition. Note that this approach can also be effective in vivo (live as opposed to imaginary) which is often performed with a therapist or supportive person present.

A variant of desensitization is called exposure therapy (Sue et. al, 2013). In this type of approach the client deliberately experiences the persons, places or things they have been avoiding which may or may not occur in a graduated fashion and/or with others present. For example, a female victim of abuse may choose a male therapist because they want to face their avoidance of men, or an alcoholic no longer avoids situations where alcohol is present in order to allow for greater flexibility and openness to experiences, as well as increased confidence in their ability to resist temptation.

Along a different vein, a variety of relaxation methods can be utilized to help clients turn on their parasympathetic nervous system which is associated with relaxation response. These methods are very similar in effects, as they facilitate greater awareness in the present, lower tension, and can be used as a supplement to therapeutically induced change or for self-help modification. Examples of this type of methodology include muscle relaxation, hypnosis, guided imagery, meditation and mindfulness exercises (the latter being Act-related). Relaxation responses, irrespective of the method employed, help reduce the power of avoidance forces.

Modeling therapy methods can be used effectively too. Exposure to appropriate and effective models has also been found to be beneficial in helping people overcome their avoidance (Sue, et. al., 2013). Once again, this methodology can be used in imagination or in vivo. Essentially, it involves observation of another person or persons facing the feared object that has been avoided previously. Although virtually anyone can serve as the model, this method tends to be most effective when employing a person who is seen as a role model by the client.

Self-administered or other-directed rewards have also been found to be effective in helping individuals overcome their avoidance patterns (Watson, 2007). For example, we may not allow ourselves to do what we want until we have done what we need to first. This is sometimes called a contingency management approach and can be very helpful in motivating us to follow through with things we have not been doing (i.e., overcome avoidance or procrastination). For example, we might not allow ourselves to go out to dinner or to a party until we take care of certain responsibilities or face a difficult situation. Or, we may decide to buy something for ourselves after we approach situations we have been avoiding.

Cognitive Therapies

Cognitive psychologists such as Ellis (1989) and Beck (1979) argued that distorted, illogical and irrational beliefs and perspectives underlie most psychological problems. Along this vein, we may learn to become a perfectionist because we've come to believe that it is horrible to make mistakes or reveal imperfections. Or, we may learn to avoid certain people or situations because of our exaggerated fears of disapproval, rejection, hurt, etc. Anxiety and fear are only one subset of emotional factors that may be avoided in this way. Shame, embarrassment, guilt, jealousy, envy, anger as well as other emotions can be associated with irrational beliefs and perspectives also. Cognitive therapists point out how the client demonstrates irrational perspectives, along with how more logical and realistic thinking may be utilized to replace these self-defeating belief systems. The therapist may or may not link the client's changes in thinking to reductions in avoidance patterns but, nevertheless, that is typically what happens.

Cognitive therapies can be quite beneficial with treating depression. For example, Beck (1979) pointed out that individuals with chronic depression tend to exhibit what he called the cognitive triad. This triad consists of three elements which are somewhat congruent with the acceptance schema put forth in this book. In simple terms, Beck's triadic elements refer to Self; "I'm worthless, Others; you're no good, and Life; living sucks." The therapist confronts the client as to whether or not these premises do in fact make sense. Over time and treatment most patients come to agree that they have positive qualities, at least some people are good, and life is a mixture of many positive and negative features.

A variant of this type of approach is based on attribution theory (Aronson, 2013). Attribution approaches help move patients from seeing their depression as stable (relatively permanent), internally caused (due to my attributes) and global (generalized qualities) toward the opposite (temporary, external, and specific). In other words, when our state of depression is viewed as stable, the result of our own making, and all encompassing, we are in psychological quick sand and see no way out. On the other hand when we accept that, at least to some extent, our depression is temporary, situational, and we are not depressed about everything, then optimism, hope and motivation to improve is enhanced and avoidance patterns tend to decrease substantially along with depression.

Glasser's (1998) Choice Theory approach basically contends that we can only directly control our own thoughts and actions. We do not and cannot control others or life situations. Further, attempts to control what is not in our purview will likely be met with opposition, rebellion and/or conflict, further adding to our anxiety and frustration in a self-defeating and exacerbating manner. So, he argues that we often need to accept the limitations imposed on us by human nature and focus on what we can control. Essentially, he emphasizes the critical impact of our choices on the consequences that accrue, positive and negative, for which we alone are responsible. With respect to depression, he stresses chronically depressed people tend to choose to be depressed. He points out that this orientation is supported by our propensity to discuss and view depression as a condition we passively tolerate. More specifically, tolerance is reflected in communication patterns such as: "John suffers from depression;" "Janet is depressed;" "Frank needs to take his medicine or he can't cope." Glasser emphasizes how differently depression is viewed with; "John chooses to depress himself." Subtly but significantly, perceptions turn when individuals are perceived as suffering from the consequences of their choices or lack thereof. They are more likely viewed as responsible for improving their condition (or not). True, situational factors may be responsible for precipitating depression but the maintenance of it is likely related to choices that amount to some degrees of avoidance and lack of acceptance. At this point, many may ask "Why would someone want to remain depressed?" Note that just because a person is chronically depressed doesn't mean they want remain in this state. As Glasser suggested, they are probably choosing depression as opposed to some other negative emotional state (i.e., suppression for anger, substitution for anxiety or fear, conversion to self-blame or punishment, or receipt of "secondary gains" such as attention, sympathy, monetary benefits, and/or avoidance of responsibilities). Note that Glasser's contention that depression can be a transformation from other emotional states is consistent with the model proposed in this book.

Humanistic Counseling

Humanistic approaches, like the client centered one developed by Carl Rogers (1959) focus on building the self-concept. Therapists provide a relationship grounded in unconditional positive regard conveyed to the client. Thus, the client receives consistent doses of warmth, acceptance and genuineness via the therapist. The unconditional positive regard received by the patient is believed to help increase their self-esteem (self-acceptance), authenticity, openness, and adaptability. This approach is devoid of specific techniques but can be very effective, particularly with people who already possess a reasonable degree of psychological health. An alternative approach to help with self-esteem enhancement will be discussed later in this chapter. The humanistic approach can help people reduce the tendency to utilize escape behaviors as a form of distraction from painful realities, such as inferiority, death, loneliness, job loss, and stressful decisions and responsibilities.

Psychodynamic Therapies

These approaches suggest that deep seated and typically unconscious forces drive our psychological conflicts and dilemmas. A main aim of this type of therapy is increased insight into the dynamics driving the self-defeating behaviors. Increased insight is deemed vital to accept how the past is linked with present feelings and thoughts, in order to be able to work through the impasse created by unconscious conflicts. In other words, from this viewpoint our present behavior problems are often rooted in our past and insight into this connection can help us change positively. This methodology offers potential insight into core issues that helped cause avoidance problems in the first place, including defense mechanisms that presumably inhibit or distort memory, such as denial, repression, projection, etc. It is presumed that avoidant and escape behaviors often keep individuals away from painful memories and insights. For example, drug and alcohol abuse and other so-called addictive behavior patterns (e.g., sexual, drug, gambling) may distract us and/or dull the senses, thereby acting as a form of escape behavior.

Existential Counseling

Existential approaches are at the forefront of those that attack purpose-related issues. As you will see, value clarification and motivational interviewing are important off-shoots of this general approach. Existential counselors do not utilize specific therapeutic techniques. Rather, this type of counseling is more of a philosophy based on existential theories. The basic tenant is that we are born into uncertainty which eventually causes existential anxiety. Further, it is theorized that we alone are responsible for our choices to move through anxiety and fears or not. Running from existential anxiety routinely is seen as causing existential guilt which is a vague sense that we're not becoming the person we want to be. According to existentialists, we find the courage to choose to move through existential anxiety through the realization that we are not alone. Fears of abandonment and separation anxiety, which includes death, are inevitable parts of the human condition which we all experience (May, 1970). Also, we find strength with strong senses of purpose and meaning in life, particularly with respect to stress and suffering. Fears of abandonment are lessened considerably via authentic encounters with one or more people which allow for sharing of the realization that we all live in an ocean of stress and unpredictability. It should be mentioned that most support groups, like Alcoholics Anonymous, are led by laypersons who essentially utilize existential approaches. AA sponsors and other members have experienced similar backgrounds and plights and, as a result, help form a cohesive group which helps members feel less alone, alienated and afraid. This helps allow them to confront their anxieties and commit to goals consistent with a set of constructive purposes and values. Also, adherence to a "Higher Power" can help them be guided by a set of beliefs and values that transform their lives into something more meaningful and coherent than they were previously.

Adjunctive Treatment Methods

There are a number of traditional methods that have wide applicability, irrespective of theoretical approach. They are discussed in the sections that follow, beginning with values clarification.

Values Clarification

There's a principle in Buddhism called Dharma. One way to conceptualize Dharma is via a jigsaw puzzle (Covey, 1989). Imagine in each of us is a specific piece of an enormous puzzle of several billion pieces. Further, consider your own personal piece of this gigantic puzzle is a specific size and shape and fits correctly in one precise place of the puzzle. Your piece of this puzzle does not fit in any other place. In other words, you are not able to be another puzzle piece; you can only be your own. Dharma teaches us that when you find out what your puzzle piece is all about, you find satisfaction in life and feel fulfilled, content and worthwhile. However, if you wander aimlessly about without establishing your puzzle piece and where it fits, or try to be someone else's piece, you will experience confusion and despair. What happens when we live according to our own puzzle piece? The natural consequences are inner peace, wisdom and contentment. We feel fulfilled and satisfied with ourselves and the direction our life is going when we are confident about our identity. What happens when we don't discover our purpose for being? What are the consequences of not knowing our inner nature and following someone else's way which is not designed for us?

Anthony Robbins (1991) describes what tends to happen when people don't take a good look at who they are and where they are going. He calls this phenomenon the Niagara Syndrome which is described as follows: "Life is like a river, and most people jump on the river of life without ever really deciding where they want to end up. So, in a short period of time, they get caught up in the current: current events, current fears, and current challenges. When they come to forks of the river, they don't consciously decide where they want to go, or which direction is right for them. They merely go with the flow. They become a part of the mass of people who were directed by the environment instead of by their own values. As a result, they feel out of control. They remain in this unconscious state until one day the sound of the raging water awakens them and they discover that they are 5 feet from Niagara Falls in a boat with no oars. At this point, all they can say is oh shoot! But by then it's too late. They are going to take a fall. Sometimes it's an enormous fall. Sometimes it's a physical fall. Sometimes it's a financial fall. It is likely that whatever challenges you have in your life currently could've been avoided by some better decisions upstream (pp. 41-42).

When we know what is important to us, decision-making and commitment become easier. Knowing our values and learning to live by them is a powerful way to gain inner peace and decrease stress levels. In order to move our behavior more in line with our values, there are several prerequisite beliefs that need to be accepted and followed (Rokeach, 1973).

1. We must believe that we are capable of changing. Regardless of our current situation, we have the capacity and ability to make changes we feel are appropriate.

2. We must believe we alone are responsible to create long-term change in our lives. Nobody else is going to do it for us. It requires our own decision, motivation and action.

3. We must believe that if we set our sights in a new direction, and move confidently in that direction, we will successfully arrive at or near the place we wanted to go.

4. We must be certain that our values determine our actions and behaviors. We may not be clear about what we value, but our choices are dependent on what we feel is most important to us. In other words, all decision-making is based on values clarification.

There are many different exercises and metaphors that can be utilized to help increase values clarification and motivation to complete value driven goals. Covey (1989) suggests the following scenario be read while the listener has eyes closed and imagination open.

> See yourself going to the funeral of a loved one. Picture yourself driving to the funeral parlor or chapel, parking the car, and getting out. As you walk inside the building, you notice the flowers and the soft organ music. You see the faces of friends and family you pass along the way. You feel a sense of sorrow that permeates the room for losing this special person. You also sense the sheer joy of having known this person that radiates from the hearts of all the people there. As you walk down to the front of the room and look inside the casket, you suddenly come face-to-face with yourself. This is your own funeral and all these people have come to honor you. They are here to express

their feelings of love and appreciation for your life. As you take a seat and wait for the services to begin, you look at the program in your hand. There are to be four speakers. The first speaker is someone from your immediate family, perhaps your mom or dad, brother, sister, aunt or uncle, cousin or grandparent. The second speaker is one of your best friends, someone who is going to tell about the kind of person you were. The third speaker is from your work or an instructor in your school. The fourth is someone from your church or community organization where you have been involved in service. Now think deeply. What would you like each of the speakers to say about you and your life? What kind of son or daughter would you like their words to reflect? What kind of friend would you like to have others say you were? Were you there for others when they needed you? Did you care for them and trust them and have a deep respect for them? What would your best friend say about you at your own funeral? What about someone who is a neighbor who knows of you, but doesn't know you really well? What contributions would you like them to have said you made to other people's lives? What achievements would you want them to remember? (pp. 7-8).

Clearly, this scenario helps focus an individual on their potential legacy. In other words, how they will be remembered by others, mainly those close to them. It can help highlight the importance of purposeful actions in the future, as opposed to unfocused and unproductive efforts to control and avoid emotions in the present. An ACT adage suggests we often need to, "get out of our mind and into living." This short but poignant statement reminds us of the folly of rigidly persisting at avoidance, suppression, and efforts to understand "why" in an attempt to avoid feeling loss and/ or pain. This coping style may persist even when the situation calls for simple contact with loss (i.e., depressed feelings and thoughts). Individuals can get stuck when they engage in ineffective actions and unproductive ruminations in the context of a loss. Certainly, it is natural for us to want to avoid pain, and it can be an appropriate and natural response to certain life situations. On the other hand, it can be difficult to accept loss/pain in our "feel good" culture which includes an endless stream of models, advertisements, magazines and television shows wherein avoidant remedies are depicted as appropriate (e.g., drugs, alcohol, medication), and short-term relief is highlighted (e.g., gratuitous sex, gambling, risky behavior).

When our values are clearly defined, they can be translated into a product generally defined as goals. This is somewhat analogous to transforming an idea into an object that can be used. As Egan (2010) emphasized, goal setting is something we do all the time. As he states; "Even not setting goals is a form of goal setting." For example, if we do not decide to get in better shape, then we have made a decision to continue along the previous path, what he calls a "default goal." He goes on to say that goals mobilize resources and are a critical part of our self-regulation system. According to a large body of research summarized by Locke and Lathan (2002), goal setting empowers us in the following ways:

1. Goals help focus our attention and action.

2. Goals help mobilize our energy and effort.

3. Goals provide incentives to search for strategies to accomplish them.

4. Clear and specific goals help us increase persistence.

5. Goals are derived from and lead to a sense of purpose.

People often have difficulty in making progress toward their goals because they have been set inappropriately. Some basic guidelines for appropriate goal setting are outlined below.

1. Choose a specific goal.

> *Inappropriate* – I will lose weight.
> Appropriate – I will reduce my calorie consumption by 20% and increase exercise time by 25%.

2. Pick a measurable goal.

> *Inappropriate* – I want to be more at peace.
> Appropriate – I will regularly engage in some form of relaxation, meditation or biofeedback.

3. Select an attainable goal.

> *Inappropriate* – I will save my marriage.
> Appropriate – I will get therapeutic help and read books on how to understand and improve marital functioning.

4. Choose a realistic goal.

> *Inappropriate* – I will become a famous and wealthy author.
> Appropriate – I will complete a book and attempt to get it published.

Motivational Interviewing

Motivation is obviously the key to effective treatment in many cases. We can make amazing changes and confront incredible challenges when sufficiently motivated. Oppositely, we can accomplish little when motivated insufficiently. In medicine, people who don't want to improve or even want to die can be healed or saved with proper treatment. Such is not the case with psychological problems. If a person does not want to change, then no treatment will work. Therefore in many cases, and especially with chronically depressed individuals, mobilizing resources in motivated fashion is crucial to effective treatment. The irony of depression is that the afflicted often say they are too depressed to do that which will get them to feel better. Besides, they have difficulty imagining their efforts will make any difference in their condition or say they can't muster enough energy to try. So, clearly it can take considerable skill and appropriately timed interventions to raise motivation to sufficient levels required to overcome inertia and avoidance forces. Previously, we discussed the roles of avoidance and approach forces in motivation. These simultaneous forces can create a great deal of ambivalence in the individual. More specifically, the chronically depressed person wants to feel better but there are likely avoidance forces that are overwhelming approach ones. A relatively new method has proved effective in dealing with this type of dilemma, called motivational interviewing. Miller and Rollnick (2002) outline the four basic procedures of this approach, and they are as follows:

1. **Express empathy** - From this perspective, it is crucial that therapists empathetically accept that the client's ambivalence about changes is normal.

2. **Help bring out the discrepancy between the client's present behavior and underlying value systems** - Potentially, this effort could help the depressed individual see that his or her present actions (or lack thereof) are inconsistent with their values and being an effective parent, role model, loving spouse, etc.

3. **Explore the pros and cons of change from the perspective of the client** – The therapist does not show understanding acceptance by pushing too hard for constructive change, as clients are more likely to show increased resistance and are less likely to develop feelings of personal freedom and control. A certain amount of resistance to change is expected because with positive change comes stress related to fear of failure, increased expectations and responsibilities, anxiety related to greater uncertainty, and so forth. The bottom line, however, is the clients must choose whether to make their own life changes or not.

4. **Increase client self-efficacy** - Clients must believe that they can be effective agents of change and they can indeed produce effects in their world through actions. As clients increase their feelings of self-efficacy, they will have more confidence in their ability to create and maintain changes

in their lives which will make them more likely to take sustained and constructive action.

Assertiveness Training

Lack of appropriate assertiveness is a very common deficit amongst Avoiders. They typically avoid expressing genuine emotions, standing up for their rights, and conflict, thereby becoming depressed, withdrawn and/or passive-aggressive. This passive-aggressive style of relating tends to alienate others and lead to poor interpersonal relationships. Certainly, lack of assertiveness is self-defeating and helps to both cause and sustain chronic depression. Assertiveness training workshops and self-help books can substitute for or serve as adjuncts to individual, group or family therapy in helping people with this vital area of psychological functioning.

Awareness and Treatment of Hypersensitivity

Elizabeth Aron (1997) has written extensively about the hypersensitive person. In many ways the hypersensitive person is a classic Avoider. Because they are so sensitive to rejection, criticism and other negative reactions, they are prone to excessive experiential avoidance. Dr. Aron's book on the Hypersensitive Person covers how one might decide whether or not they meet the criteria for such, as well as how this type of interpersonal difficulty can be addressed effectively. Hypersensitive individuals are vulnerable to developing both depression and anxiety-related disorders. But, keep in mind that early diagnosis and treatment is crucial because it helps allow for more favorable prognoses. Certainly, the hypersensitive person needs to be realistic about how much they can change or even want to, as well as how much they are willing to invest in efforts to do so. The author's clinical experience suggests that these individuals can only change so much, even with a great deal of effort. Therefore, to some extent they need to embrace their individual differences, as opposed to rejecting them. Generally, they need to be okay with the reality that they are probably going to continue to be much more sensitive than the average person. If they think or feel flawed or inadequate for being hypersensitive, then they need to accept that these are just feeling and thoughts, not facts. At the same time, they need to push themselves to "face the fire" of situations they might otherwise avoid or escape from when these situations are important to their value system. If not, they are likely to be frustrated and underachieve which will eventually lead to depression. Furthermore, since it is generally easier and less stressful to alter situations than change personality, they need to more frequently put themselves in situations which make it easier for them to be authentic and feel satisfied. For example, they may operate rather well in situations wherein they are the "expert" and feel in control. Likewise, they may be most comfortable with one-on-one interactions and small groups of people they know well or with whom they share important interests and values. In essence, they need to be the best hypersensitive person they can be! Alternatively, they may want to avoid interactions with people who are excessive critical and judgmental (unless they want to practice their assertiveness!).

Self-Concept Therapy

There is little doubt that the self-concept is the most significant aspect of personality structure. It is the organizing force for our thoughts and actions. We can think of self-esteem as the evaluative aspect of our self-concept. In other words, aspects of our self-esteem reflect the ways in which we see ourselves favorably or unfavorably, good versus bad, and positive versus negative. This writer's clinical experience suggests that chronically depressed people almost invariably possess low self-esteem in pivotal aspects of their self-concept. This is not surprising when we consider the impact of low self-esteem on various domains. Low self-esteem can help create self-fulfilling prophecies in which we defeat ourselves before even out of the starting gate. In other words, why should I try when I'm quite sure I will fail? Moreover, effective interpersonal relationships become almost impossible when we think we are unlikable or unlovable. People with low self-esteem find it very difficult to believe that someone else truly likes or loves them. As a result, they tend to be very self-defeating in relationships. Self-defeat can occur in a number of ways. For example, we could end a relationship because we have determined that the other party must be a fool to see us in such positive light. Or, we may terminate contact because we have decided that the other individual simply doesn't know us well yet but, when they do, will reject us. Therefore, why should we waste our time and theirs'? The prudent thing is to quit while the quitting is good. Of course, the other path to cognitive consistency is to prove the other person is correct in their judgment by behaving in inappropriate ways and/or tolerating being taken advantage of. Thus, people with low self-esteem are prone to getting into and staying in relationships that are at best unsatisfying and fraught with wrangles and, at worst, psychologically and/or physically abusive. Certainly, this makes it much more likely for them to experience depression and have difficulty getting out of this state and the situations causing it.

There are a plethora of self-help books on the power of positive thinking. Unfortunately, for the individual suffering from key aspects of low self-esteem, these books are relatively worthless. Research is clear in showing that repetitive practice in making positive self-statements can be helpful for those already high in self-esteem but not for those low in this construct (Wood et. al., 2000). Individuals who are already high on themselves tend to find positive self-statements reinforcing and even motivational with respect to goal directed behavior. Conversely, low self-esteem persons tend to experience further decrements in the areas targeted by their positive self-referent statements. Admittedly, this is a perplexing finding and we are not entirely sure of the cause(s). However, questioning of research participants reveals that when they rehearse positive self-esteem thoughts inconsistent with how they actually think about themselves, it makes them feel worse. In other words, such thoughts are incongruent with their present (real) self and induce them to be painfully aware of how discrepant they are from their ideal self.

This author has developed a structured approach to self-esteem enhancement that has been quite useful for many clients. Clients are asked to draw a pie chart of their main roles and personal characteristics (e.g., physical, intellectual, spiritual, emotional, intellectual, citizenship, friendship, employee, parent, etc.). Then, they are asked to color or shade in the areas in which they judge themselves adequate/satisfactory or better. This part of the exercise helps them realize that they do not have generically low self-esteem. Note that this clinician has never had one individual who failed to color in at least a few areas in which they felt adequate. On the other hand, this psychologist has had many individuals make a statement to the effect that: "I have no self-esteem." Thus, in coloring or shading certain key aspects of themselves, they have just provided confirmation that they have some aspects of positive self-esteem. Then, they are encouraged to work on the uncolored areas of most priority to them. Note that they are encouraged to follow the guidelines proposed previously with goal setting. The bottom line is that we cannot expect our self-esteem to increase without changing behaviors related to the aspect being targeted. Put another way, it is hard for us to argue with our own results. When we see that we have been able to take charge and change certain behaviors, it gives us a boost in confidence and evidence to support new attitudes about ourselves. It seems that there is nothing better than getting a hit in terms of raising our self-esteem. We can think all we want about getting a hit but there is no substitute for increasing our self-esteem like actually getting one. If we continue to get up to the plate and swing, then sooner or later we are bound to get a hit. The consequences of getting a hit with regard to self-esteem enhancement appear to dwarf the effects of positive thinking for people low in self-esteem. Certainly, there can be important developmental shifts and some people can go from low to high or vice versa across several domains as they age. For example, physical appearance is generally an extremely significant aspect of self-esteem when people are teenagers and young adults. It tends to diminish during the adulthood years while other aspects grow stronger (e.g., earning power, education, intellect, health, etc.). People may need to be reminded that aspects of self-esteem important to them now may not be at a later date and vice versa.

Summary and Conclusions

In conclusion, there been many studies showing that traditional cognitive-behavior (CBT) therapy can be quite effective in dealing with a wide range of psychological problems, including depression. At the same time, more recent research also supports the effectiveness of ACT, with outcomes generally equaling or bettering those obtained with CBT (Hayes & Strosahl, 2010). Although many people respond well to traditional CBT, individuals with complex and chronic cases often do not. Many professionals believe that ACT is better suited to these types of cases.

Perhaps, this is partly due to the blending of numerous therapies with ACT, as it involves an integration of existential/gestalt, cognitive and behavioral therapies (CBT), Eastern methods (e.g., mindfulness), etc. As such, it may be that the strict rational/logical approach of traditional CBT simply misses the point for some people. For example, some may need a more insight oriented approach. Some may need to attack their issues on a more emotional level. And, some may need help with the direction and clarity of their values and purposes in life. Finally, some may be looking for a fix or cure that doesn't exist and could benefit from a large dose of acceptance approaches. Whatever the case, is encouraging to know that there are a variety of therapeutic modalities available and it one size does not fit all. From the perspective of this book, regardless of the theoretical and therapeutic orientations taken, experiential avoidance will need to be addressed in most cases in order to effectuate optimal therapeutic progress. Moreover, it is argued here that the success of all therapies depends largely on how motivated the client is to face their avoidance and acceptance issues, as well as the therapist's skill in helping them get on and stay on these paths.

Chapter Five

Case Study Examples

These cases are representative of the kind this author has seen while performing many years of psychotherapy. As you will see, although the content varies considerably across the patients discussed, the underlying processes are quite similar. We all struggle with change and uncertainty, including fears of abandonment, daily hassles and unexpected blows, as well as mustering the persistence and fortitude required to reach important milestones and achievements. Just when we think that we have all the bases covered, life has a way of throwing another curve at us. These cases were chosen because they reflect real life challenges of people who struggled, successfully or unsuccessfully, with facing major responsibilities and decisions, most particularly whether or not to avoid or face the challenges of psychological adaptation and growth. Along these lines, these cases highlight what happens when we run from our problems. Like a house that is not maintained, problems continue to mount and expand when not addressed expeditiously. Eventually, they can reach an overwhelming point, as we and others associated with us can only take so much. We lose confidence in ourselves when this path is taken and, almost assuredly, become more depressed along the way. The cases that follow demonstrate how confronting important decisions, changes, responsibilities and pain can yield positive outcomes and growth. The names used in the cases have been changed, and many of the demographics (e.g., gender, number of children, age) were altered too in order to preserve anonymity. Finally, place of residence, job, etc. were purposely referenced in general or altered so as to protect the identity of the individuals discussed in the Case Studies.

Included with some of the Case Studies are examples of hypothetical scenarios (see one below) that have been utilized with these and other clients in attempts to help drive home therapeutic interventions involving aspects of avoidance, acceptance and purposeful action. This type of strategy is consistent with the use of so-called metaphors applied by ACT-therapists. Sometimes they are used in conjunction with relaxation exercises as a form of guided imagery. Other clients may be more comfortable with an eyes open, direct communication approach. Some clients use these images as "homework" assignments. Typically, this is done voluntarily and at their own discretion. Often, they may only need a one trial experience to get the "message" loud and clear.

A case in point can be made with the example of Ramona in Chapter Two. Recall that Ramona had a chronic pain condition due to a car accident. She went into a shell and was no longer the person, wife and mother she was before the accident and certainly not living life consistent with her value system. A scenario resembling the Titanic can prove very beneficial in this type of situation.

Imagine you are on the Titanic and a member the ship's orchestra. Tragically, and consistent with history, the cruise ship is going down. You learn that there are not enough lifeboats for the crew and understand you have very little time to live. There is no way to contact your family on shore. What are you thinking and what are you to do? Historical accounts tell us that many members of the band continued to play on even as the ship was slowly sinking. These individuals did not panic or try to get on lifeboats before or instead of women and children. They remained steadfast with their values, duty and ethical standards under one of the most difficult situations imaginable. They eked out as much pleasure and meaning from life as possible, knowing they had precious little time remaining. They controlled what they could and managed to let go of what they could not. Can you imagine getting every possible amount of pleasure and meaning out of life in this type of situation? Can you imagine acting with such character when the chips are so down? Do you act like the band members? If not, are you willing to commit to doing so in the future?

The Five Avoider Types

A case study for each Avoider Type follows first. Then, each combination of Self, Other and Life Acceptance-type difficulties are covered. Finally, two cases where little or minimal therapeutic support were required are discussed.

Runner

Andy grew up in a relatively normal family until one tragic day. He was playing on the ice when his sister fell into frozen lake water. He tried to save her but couldn't hold onto her hand. His sister died that day and Andy's life changed forever. He could neither rid himself of the loss and guilt associated with this tragedy nor live up to the idealism to which his sister was exalted in his mind. Of course, he and others could imagine his sister to be an almost perfect human being "if she had just lived." He suffered from the perception that he could never live up to this billing. Eventually, it was hard for him to escape the notion that the wrong sibling died. Still, during his teenage and young adult years he tried to prove his worthiness and worked hard to distract himself from painful memories of the tragic loss of his sister.

Andy was bright and talented. He excelled at school, graduated from college and then began climbing the career ladder. At the same time, he met a young gal and they started a family. On the surface, everything seemed fine. However, beneath the still water lurked deep seated feelings of low self-esteem and depression. Since his sister's death, he developed a perspective that he did not deserve happiness. Whenever he experienced happiness, he felt ambivalence because of guilt. Ambivalence helped drive him to escape via compulsive acts of self-destruction, manifested mainly in excessive drinking. During these episodes, he alienated others with his alcohol abuse and related behaviors. This caused others to reject these behaviors which reinforced his aspects of low self-esteem. Eventually, this led to the breakup of his marriage and family life, including strained relationships with his children. In addition, he made so many major mistakes in his chosen profession that he could not keep a decent paying job. Therefore, he changed to another line of work which paid less and kept him away from his family most nights. Moreover, his new line of work was paraprofessional and allowed him more latitude in terms of work-related behavior. Put another way, he could miss work periodically and even drink while at his place of employment.

Eventually, he met a career woman with several children who fell in love with his potential; a risky decision on her part. She didn't see the danger of this approach, especially given the fact that he had struggled with his issues for several decades. She imagined that they could be the Brady Bunch but that was not to be. Although things started out well, they soon became rocky as Andy's drinking accelerated. True to form, as he started to get more satisfied with this life, his drinking and other self-destructive behavior patterns accelerated.

His wife strongly encouraged him to go to counseling, see a psychiatrist, and attend AA meetings. It soon became clear Andy's alcohol abuse was the primary way he self-medicated. Although he knew alcohol abuse was a symptom of underlying issues, it was also an extremely entrenched lifestyle. It was a coping strategy that helped him get relief temporarily while masking his underlying core problems and creating new ones. Unfortunately, his internal conflicts were not faced earlier in life when they were more amenable to change. Success in this regard could have prevented much pain in his and others' lives but he failed to get proper assistance earlier. He had primarily taken a medicinal approach to his problems. However, there was no medication that could erase the memories, pain or ambivalence he experienced. Besides, the medication he chose was alcohol. He couldn't run from or erase his past but he could have come to accept it.

As it turned out, Andy went for help too late. He lost his job and never returned to work. He had reached the end of the line. Even the government believed he could not work full-time, as he received social security disability benefits. The many psychiatric medications he was tried on, not surprisingly, proved ineffective. Ultimately, his second wife told him she could no longer take his shenanigans and asked him to leave.

He moved into an apartment by himself. Andy allowed himself to be reduced to a self-pitying and masochistic individual, self- preoccupied and disconnected from everyone. He gave up on his individual counseling, AA meetings and psychiatric medications.

Unfortunately, as we know, not all stories have happy endings. It was not long after their marital separation that and he took his life. Perhaps, in his mind he finally joined his sister. At any rate, he ended the pain of his guilt and chronic depression. Unfortunately, he never accepted that his sister's death was neither his fault nor something he could control. Although Andy had many reasons to live and fight through his demons, he came to believe that he was only encumbering others with his lack of responsibility and alcoholism. These maladaptive coping styles created a great deal of shame which enhanced his tendency to withdraw, deceive and keep secrets. Thus, he was caught in a vicious cycle. He couldn't get over his conflicts without facing his shame and guilt. However, the shame and guilt prevented him from opening and dealing with his underlying issues and pain. He was between the devil and the deep blue sea. Although he felt trapped and immobilized in pain, there was a way out. He needed to face the pain of dealing with his old nemesis. It would be extremely difficult but it was the only exit for continued existence and life worth living. He came to feel that his wife and family were better off without him. Of course, he came to this belief because of the behavior patterns he engaged in for many years. His alternative was to change his self-destructive patterns. But, to do so, he would have had to have to face and accept the tragedy of his sister's death and find ways to travel responsibly through life's ups and downs.

Although Andy is classified here as a Runner, which was his primary and early form of avoidance, he developed characteristics of the Denier, Irresponsible and Escape Artist over many years of self-defeating coping styles. These four patterns were relatively well established by the time he entered therapy, along with his very poor self-concept. As for acceptance issues, he clearly displayed patterns of being Self-Centered, Self-Debasing and Unforgiving with respect to Self. With regard to others, he was Alienating so as to not let anyone get too close to him while showing strong aspects of being Nonreciprocal, Pessimistic, Rigid and Meaningless with respect to Life.

Unfortunately, his therapy stint was brief and too little too late. He didn't possess enough purpose to allow him to confront significant others and stressors, despite the support he received from his wife and the importance of having children and stepchildren who depended on and cared for him. He had succeeded at alienating himself from those who gave him a second chance. He provides a good example of how much can be achieved with sufficient motivation and how little without it. There is little we cannot do if we set our mind to it whereas even small tasks and accomplishments seem insurmountable when our motivation is minimal. In the end he convinced himself that significant others would be better off without him which helped justify taking the ultimate path of avoidance, suicide. As a result, he no longer had to face his inability to forgive/accept himself.

Denier

Paul came into marital counseling after many years of being treated for Bipolar Disorder. He had been married for over 30 years and there were several adult children from his union with his wife, Pam.

Paul functioned relatively well over the years while on lithium. He was reliable and hardworking in the construction field. Pam was a college graduate and worked as a professional. After many years on lithium, this psychiatric medication created some serious side effects which led him to take a different mood stabilizer. This was a difficult adjustment for both Paul and Pam, as he was more moody and irritable as a result. They were concerned that he might have to go into a psychiatric facility as he had several times during their marriage. Paul was even alienating his adult children with intrusive proselytizing and lectures. Eventually, he was stabilized on a new set of medications.

Both Paul and Pam agreed that their kids had been: "The glue that kept them together." Their adult children had created their own families and were doing quite well. So, it was now just Paul and Pam in a home that Paul essentially built. Paul and Pam spent minimal quality time together. When Pam had time, she usually spent it with members of her family of origin and/or their kids. Paul spent a lot of time at home and liked to work on projects such as home improvements, woodworking, etc. He had a tendency to be perfectionistic in his work on the job and home. Most people would probably classify him as a workaholic. He often bragged about how long and hard he could work and how he was stronger and more capable than most of his co-workers. When they did spend time together, they usually got into some type of conflict. The disagreements usually took the same form. Paul would try to engage Pam in some type of contact, intimate or otherwise. She would typically ignore him, give him short and direct answers or attack him with profanity. Paul didn't use profanity and wasn't comfortable with arguing. He didn't believe it solved anything. So, her responses tended to shut him up. He developed strong ties with their children, as did Pam.

Fundamentally, Paul was a very religious man who possessed strong needs for nurturance and affection. He came from a large, close-knit family that promoted competition, independence and success. Pam came from a small, non-demonstrative family atmosphere that promoted independence also.

Paul admitted that there was never much "chemistry" in their marriage which he denied from the start. He stated early in the counseling process that Pam didn't want to be intimate on their honeymoon. As he stated; "She was never that into me." Both agreed that their sex life had been a bust which was okay with Pam. She did want an intimate relationship with Paul or seemingly anyone for that matter. Pam was a practical, tough-minded individual who basically wanted a partner to help raise children with, along with establishing a career of her own. These were sufficient goals for her but not Paul. They conflicted over fundamental values and personality differences for many years. His main underlying issue was always the same. He felt frustrated and rejected in terms of the love and intimacy received from Pam.

While the kids were growing up, Paul was able to get some basic emotional needs met through relationships with them. Also, he worked tirelessly in his job and on building their dream home. These activities helped displace his thoughts and energies away from frustrations with Pam. However, as the kids grew older and his house projects were complete, his attention returned to what he saw and felt to be a stagnant and loveless marriage. The switch from lithium to other medications eventually helped him feel more stable, focused and confident. So, he decided to get into marital counseling upon the advice of his psychiatrist. Eventually, this helped him to view his current state of depression in relation to his marital problems.

Unfortunately, marital counseling did not lead to an ideal outcome. Both were very recalcitrant in their lifestyles and postures. It became obvious that they had grown into a reversal of traditional sex stereotyped roles. Pam was acting like the tough-minded, dominant male who complained of being nagged. Paul, on the other hand, had slipped into a role of the imploring woman who was dissatisfied with lack of attention and intimacy. After a few months of marital counseling, it became clear the sessions did little more than offer a forum for them to argue in more humane fashion than would occur at home. Pam stopped coming and Paul continued individual counseling to help with his frustration, loneliness and depression.

Throughout the next year so, Paul continued to complain about Pam while refusing to change his perspectives or behaviors. Eventually, Pam left Paul and lived in a family owned residence. Occasionally, she returned home briefly for convenience sake. Nevertheless, her attitudes and behaviors toward Paul worsened, although she expressed no desire to divorce. As time passed, Paul's physical and emotional well-being deteriorated. Predictably, as his complaints mounted, his psychiatrist repeatedly changed and/or raised his medications which caused him to be in a zombie-like state much of the time. He began to have trouble walking, experienced blurry vision, complained of poor concentration, and exhibited hand tremors. Finally, one of the sisters came on the scene and pushed him get better control of his life. Although his counselor had been trying to get him to make needed changes, he resisted. However, his sister was relentless and even went with him to numerous doctor appointments, including psychotherapy ones. She insisted that he get a thorough neurological workup and spoke with his psychiatrist about his medications.

These efforts led to a number of important changes, as medical exams were negative. This finding gave credence to the notion that his psychiatric medications were likely the culprit of a number of troubling side effects. Reduction in these medications helped him get his old personality back. He still had some very slight hand tremors due to the mood stabilizer medication but his other symptoms all but disappeared. His concentration and memory increased significantly. He no longer acted like someone suffering from dementia. His bland facial expression was gone and he was able to drive again because his vision returned to previous levels of acuity. Moreover, once his energy and enthusiasm returned, he was ready to finally tackle his Achilles heel, avoidance of certain realities. For decades, he had been running from the truth. He refused to face that, considering his personality needs, he married the wrong type of person. Of course, it was particularly difficult to accept this reality once they had children and he built a home for the family. However, he was coming to accept that they had been only married nominally. Along this vein, he was able to state that, Psychologically and spiritually, they were never married. As a result, for the first time he was able to fully accept their marital separation and that it was natural for him to want female companionship from someone other than his wife. This didn't mean he was a "bad person." His deep religious convictions had made it extremely difficult to accept these feelings and perspectives. Also, he saw how his refusals to accept the truths of their relationship caused much of his psychological suffering and damage.

It took another couple of years, but he finally met a terrific woman with a very different personality. They were much more simpatico and brought out the best in one another. They had great conversations and shared many interests. He may never get married again but that's okay with him. He is no longer contorting himself to someone else's personality. He accepts himself and the reality of his relationships. Paul over-utilized denial as a defensive posture. Understandably, we all use denial to varying degrees. It can help give us time to accept difficult realities. However, the excessive use of denial, as we have evidenced with Paul, will almost certainly get us into trouble. A scenario that can be useful with this type of therapeutic situation follows.

> An elderly blind woman felt an open sore one day on her knee. She didn't think much of it but asked a family member to put a band aid on it. Over time the sore didn't heal. As a matter of fact, it gradually grew to the point that a large band aid would not cover it. Her family implored her to go to the doctor to find out what the problem was but

she kept saying it was nothing and they shouldn't worry. After about a year, the sore was growing larger at a faster rate and the gauze the family was putting on the sore was about six inches wide. Family members insisted she go to her doctor and she finally relented. Medical tests revealed a slow growing cancer. Unfortunately, it had traveled into her lymph system because she waited a long time to get it diagnosed. It wasn't too long thereafter she agonizingly died from cancer. Doctors told the family that, if she had come in earlier for diagnosis and treatment, the cancer most likely would have been successfully eradicated. The point here is that getting a diagnosis didn't change the reality of what was growing inside her body. Denial, in terms of not looking for the truth, allowed her to delay facing the fact of what was causing her sore. Clearly the unintended consequences of denial can be horrific. Does denial play a significant role in your life? If so, how and what can you do about it? Are you willing and committed to make appropriate changes?

Interestingly, it took a great deal of time and pain for Paul to finally stop avoiding the truth. He put it off for over 30 years. However, it was his only path out of the psychological hell he backed himself into and tolerated for so long. His willingness to confront the realities of his life helped him make different choices. He chose to no longer fight battles he could not win. He chose to put his energies into constructive pursuits that had a better chance of bringing him greater life satisfaction in the present and future. Eventually, this facilitated the transformation of negative emotions into positive motivation and behavior. The transformation was manifested in him starting his own business as a part time maintenance and handyman. As his business became successful, he experienced greater senses of purpose and productivity which further enhanced his self-esteem and life satisfaction. He didn't need to change his values. He needed to redirect his energies into a different set of priorities. Raising the children, building a home and commitment to his marriage were no longer valued or paying off.

In terms of acceptance issues, Paul showed strong indications of being Perfectionistic and Self-Centered in relation to Self, Alienating, Reactive and Naïve in association with Others, and Rigid and Simplistic in Life orientation. Fortunately, he was eventually capable and motivated with regard to confronting these issues. Certainly, his deep religious values and volunteer activities at his Church were helpful with his acceptance struggles. Eventually, he came to see how he simplistically and rigidly held to the belief that medication (alone) would heal his "sickness." He came to accept how naïve he was to believe that his unaffectionate wife would change or never leave him, unless he gave her some dramatic and unforgiving justification. He came to empathize with friends and family in terms of how his dogmatic attempts at getting others to agree with and live by his value systems alienated them. These acceptances helped "soften" his personality style and made him more approachable and less lonely and depressed.

Blamer

Ron grew up in a traditional Catholic family. His parents were conventional people who worked hard to provide well for their family which included Ron and a younger sister. Ron's sister was the typical girl next door who was balanced and easy to parent. Ron was a good student but the type that other kids found to be "weird," a characterization that even his family agreed with. During the years he was in school, Ron was diagnosed with an anxiety disorder and narcissistic (entitled) personality, although he also showed signs of autism. As a result, he often behaved inappropriately and others viewed his as a nuisance. He tried extremely hard to make friends but was unsuccessful. He was continuously lonely and frustrated growing up. After many years of feeling this way, he became a "Blamer." He complained excessively about how others were rude, insensitive, hostile and uncaring. Nevertheless, he was obsessed with dating and finding a mate. He failed to see the roles he had been playing for so many years and how unsuccessful he had been with his aggressive strategies.

His lack of insight and acceptance were understandable to some degree. His parents were not frank with him about what they saw and tended to tacitly agree with his narcissistic complaints. They failed to point out what was obvious; there was something wrong with the way he was "wired." It is as though he was born with a learning disability that did not allow him to naturally understand social discourse. To make matters worse, before he started sessions with the author, he met for about a year with a clinical psychologist who led him down a wrong turn. While in college, his therapist required that he ask out three co-eds per week for a date or he would not see him for their next visit. This strategy was utilized for seven months before the ludicrous approach was mercifully curtailed. During that time, he asked out about 100 young women, most of whom he didn't even know but attended the same small college. They often responded to him like he was from another planet. He was successful at one thing, developing a negative reputation at his college! Only three of the co-eds accepted a date and only one actually showed up. Not surprisingly, they didn't become a couple!

Upon getting involved in therapy with this clinician, focus turned to what others, including Ron, were ignoring; that is, his obvious and severe predisposition towards deficient social skills. Ron was not only clueless with respect to social discourse, he learned little from his failures, inappropriateness and the rejection he received.

A good deal of time was spent on helping advance his social skills. Goal setting was altered significantly. The shotgun approach used by the other psychologist was abandoned and a more targeted one put in place. Ron came to agree that it would be better to ask out several women he came to know casually and get a hit rate of two or three (live ones) than continue with his doomed-to-failure method. Ron gradually came to accept that he was quite different from his peers. He could only be the best Ron he could be. As he came to accept his unique and special nature, his anger subsided and he stopped trying to control his social world. There wasn't a Disneyworld ending. Now in middle age, he still does not have a companion but works in the professional world and lives independently. He works out at the gym regularly and takes good care of his personal hygiene and physical health. He is relatively content with his social and family life and, after many years of professional and self-help, Ron is no longer a Blamer.

The therapeutically-derived acceptances in Ron no longer allow him to continue to avoid the realities of his uniqueness. Ron realizes now that he tried to create a positive social and emotional life outside of his family of origin without the requisite patience, attitudes and social skills. He struggled with understanding and accepting why his life didn't smoothly and quickly progress in the ways he wanted during college and beyond. With respect to Self, Ron believed he was entitled to date gals of his dreams simply because he was a relatively good looking, hard –working, nice guy. Clearly, he underestimated the competitiveness of social dating and mating which revealed Grandiose and Self-Centered aspects of Self. With regard to Others, he proved to be Alienating, Impractical, Naïve and Reactive (emotionally) when he frequently didn't get his way. Finally, acceptance issues with Life were exemplified with his Noncreative, Rigid and Simplistic styles. Rather than exhibiting patience with his social maturation, he stuck to Simplistic and Dependent styles of coping (i.e., what his initial therapist told him to do), despite overwhelming and consistent evidence that his approaches were not only unsuccessful but backfiring in terms of giving him a negative reputation around campus, increasing his frustration and lowering his self-esteem. In essence he wishfully believed in a simple answer to a complex issue which is a common and self-defeating fallacy. As we often see in retrospect, if things seem very simple or easy, then they are probably too good to be true. Fortunately, he engaged in long term therapy which helped him counteract his avoidance and acceptance problems while giving him more time and opportunity to be more realistic in his endeavors to change what he could influence or control more directly.

Irresponsible

Ernesto grew up in a traditional Italian family. He was the youngest of five siblings. His early years in school were unremarkable, except that he began to show signs of attention deficit disorder. Ernesto developed a reputation of a "goof ball" and was regularly a scapegoat at home and school. He learned to retreat into his own fantasy world which only made things worse for him. Not surprisingly, he developed generically low self-esteem and ran with the wrong crowd during junior high and high school. Like many ADHD kids, he was the "Jack of all trades and master of none," except music. He mastered the keyboard by young adulthood without any formal training. His musical talents brought him into many late-night clubs with drug and alcohol abusers, as well as fast women who followed the bands he played with. His ADHD-related impulsivity, along with the emotional deprivation he grew up with, made him vulnerable to developing drug abuse patterns. After years of "wine, women and song," he met a young woman who set out to tame him. Although he told her that he didn't want children and had no intention of quitting the band, they decided to marry.

In the meantime his dad's passing caused a great deal of financial strain on the family. His brothers became consumed with making up for the loss of family income, as well as the development of their own careers. They became extremely successful in the business world and could be described as workaholics. The discrepancy between his brother's personalities and his own served to push Ernesto further away from his family of origin.

Although his wife helped keep Ernesto away from drugs and alcohol and oriented toward a "real job," she also discouraged him from his first love, music. He came to resent what he considered his wife's control of his life. Occasionally, this fostered his passive-aggressive acting out with drugs. Consequently, his wife would lash out at him and sometimes call his brothers in order to get them to straighten him out by condemning him into shame. Eventually, one of his brothers gave him a low level position in his business which was a double-edged sword. On the one hand, it helped Ernesto and his wife with the family bills. However, it didn't help Ernesto's frustration with giving up his music or with his low self-esteem. Working for his brother helped make him feel more like a loser and a child again.

During the next couple of decades, Ernesto engaged in outpatient psychotherapy and psychiatry with many providers, and was hospitalized for drug and alcohol and mental health treatment on numerous occasions. Unfortunately, he tended to look at medication as a solution and sometimes abused prescription medications. This led to doctors refusing to prescribe the attention deficit and anxiety medications he needed. Despite his lack of desire for such, Ernesto gave into his wife's desire for children which tended to create more stress and conflict in the marriage. His wife worked steadily in part-time employment and Ernesto eventually received a psychiatric disability. Unfortunately, the children witnessed their mother psychologically and physically attack their father during tirades over his actual and perceived transgressions. His wife felt an enormous lack of support while he often retorted that he never wanted children in the first place. Both Ernesto and his wife showed a long-term pattern of avoiding some basic truths about their marriage which kept them in continuous battle like two rams with their horns locked.

Ernesto avoided following his true love, music. He walked away from more than one opportunity to engage in regional or national tours with a band that became highly successful and well-known. Constant reminders of his missed opportunities exacerbated depressive bouts and soured his waning desire to play music. He wanted to play locally with bands but his wife didn't trust him and he allowed her to convince him the money he wanted to spend on decent musical equipment had to be used for family bills. Her lack of trust and support increased his resentment and temptation to act out occasionally with drug use. He refused to face the reality of his self-defeating behavior patterns and failed marriage, as well as the effects of each of their children. As for his wife, she refused to accept their irreconcilable differences and how her efforts to control Ernesto were counterproductive. Her efforts to control him simply caused him to be more oppositional and rebellious. Although he only abused drugs and alcohol occasionally, his depression worsened. His disability income paid for home-related bills but there was little left over for him to pursue musical interests which, ironically, could have substantially increased their family income. The kids are almost adults now and the beneficiaries of little. They did learn how to have a dissatisfying and unworkable marriage. More specifically, they repeatedly were dragged into conflicts and power struggles which helped cause the children to feel they had to take sides and/ or withdraw. Unfortunately, they learned how to live in a marriage lacking in warmth and teamwork, and how to excessively avoid problems and engage in non-acceptance as a coping pattern. Their home became a place of pessimism and isolation in which each member of the family withdrew into their own psychological world. The kids developed fragile self-esteem, problems initiating and maintaining intimate relationships, and a strong desire to leave home for college. They did, however, develop musical talent, without much direct involvement from dad. Music helped them cope with the stress they were so accustomed to in the home environment. We can only hope that they don't become Avoiders like their parents. Ernesto has essentially given up at this point. This isn't surprising given his history of quitting on pretty much everything he ever started. Despite many years of psychiatric and psychological help, not to mention support from his family, he has finally given up his therapies and tossed in the towel. He woefully submits to his wife and lets his adult children ignore and occasionally disrespect him. Ernesto reminds us of the notion that the only way a person can truly fail is to quit. The only thing we can directly and surely control is our effort. It can make us mindful of a scenario like the one below.

> Johnny is 9 years old and plays little league. He had been fearful of the pitched ball when at bat. The first few times he went to the plate the bat never left his shoulder. His parents encouraged him to swing at the ball when he saw a good pitch. The next few times he got to the plate he swung and missed three times and struck out but his parents gave him praise for trying. The told him things like "keep it up champ, you're going to get a hit one of these times." And sure enough, it wasn't long before he starting hitting the ball and getting on base with a big smile on his face. His parents knew that, if he kept swinging, sooner or later he would get positive results. Does this theme play out in your life? Do you quit on yourself pre-maturely? Do you lose focus on the only thing you can control; your effort? How might your life be different if you didn't do these things?

Unfortunately, Ernesto gave up on himself a long time ago. He developed life-long patterns of avoiding responsibility and growth which were represented by giving up on himself and blaming his wife. He foreclosed early on his career aspirations, including the development of his musical talent and creativity. He quit on developing as a husband, father and extended family member too. Eventually, no one he knew expected much from him. Others learned to expect that Ernesto would only make half-hearted efforts before giving up once again, and he came to the same beliefs. He had observed and evaluated the same patterns in himself. Ernesto proved to be incapable of facing criticism and rejection in the music field, as well as asserting himself appropriately and effectively with his wife, children and family of origin. With respect to Life issues, his non-acceptance was reflected in thinking and acting Helpless, being Pessimistic and engaging in Meaningless activities. Of course, none of these orientations facilitated positive self-esteem or relationships. Wasting money on drugs rather than investing in his musical talents and aspirations was self-defeating and helped further alienate significant others. For example, there were occasions where he sold his only instrument to buy drugs. As of this writing, Ernesto is still struggling with the above stated acceptance issues. He is running out of hope, energy and time to make sufficient changes and he knows it. He is so demoralized after decades of his self-defeating and avoidant life style that his main hurdle is mustering the wherewithal to just squeeze by day to day. Like so many people with chronic psychological problems, he knows what he needs to do. The key is whether or not he possesses enough purpose to overcome the inertia required to face and work through the stress of changing fundamental aspects of his life. Unfortunately, motivational interviewing, attempts to restructure his self-concept, existential counseling approaches, along with ACT-like intervention were unproductive in helping him get over the hurdles required to engage in sustained purposeful action.

Escape Artist

Zane's father abandoned the family when he was just a child, and he grew up with alcoholic mother who had a gambling problem. Until young adulthood, Zane was an outgoing person who succeeded academically and socially. He developed a close relationship with one of his peers, Carl, and was pretty much adopted by Carl's family. Carl became like a brother to Zane and his father was like a surrogate father to him.

After graduating from college, Zane and Carl worked with Carl's family business. They were very successful in growing the mid-size corporation, as they were very responsible and intelligent. They intended to make the business their life's work. However, Zane possessed some underlying and potentially destructive psychological issues that had not yet come to light. Although Zane loved his wife and children and was well-respected in their community, he had serious unresolved issues from his childhood and adolescence. His sense of abandonment via his father leaving and lack of warmth and nurturance received from his mother, left him with deep in unresolved emotional issues.

Zane spent most of his life avoiding these issues and the insecurities associated with them. He lacked the insight necessary to understand the extent to which they inhibited him from sharing himself fully and trusting others. Zane seemed to be living the American dream with a nice house, healthy kids, an excellent career and loving family. Nevertheless, Zane felt empty and alone and his successes and family life were not "enough" for him. The fact is he could never have enough. The psychological hole he developed could not be filled with adult success or intimate relationships because he was too busy running from his childhood insecurities and demons.

Zane grew impatient with the steady but mild to moderate incline of his salary and the business. He began to get involved in his own get-rich-quick schemes and developed a serious gambling problem. He had grandiose fantasies of getting incredibly rich and powerful while being seen by others as brilliant and masterful. He even admitted to Carl that; "no amount of money could ever be enough for me." Zane's risky schemes and gambling gradually increased in intensity and he had to borrow large sums of money, most of which he didn't pay back. His preoccupation with gambling and marked levels of frustration alienated family members, Carl, coworkers and friends. Over more than a decade, he took advantage of many people with his gambling compulsion, including family members and Carl. As is the case with most gamblers, he was very secretive and dishonest. His life was full of deception and false promises. More than once, Zane quit his job only to return within a short period of time to ask for reinstatement. Eventually, he was told that he would not be accepted back at work. Also, bookies stopped advancing him credit and pressured him to pay up. Family and friends stopped lending him money which they came to understand would probably never be paid back. Finally, in desperation, he visited briefly with his priest and a psychologist. However, he never really fully opened up about the real nature of his gambling and psychological problems. His failure to address underlying core issues in his personality finally caught up with him, and he was being cornered by numerous major stressors. He was in danger of losing the family home and was the only person who knew this and other truths.

It is painfully ironic that Zane, who was so successful in many walks of life, felt unworthy of love and approval from others. Despite all of his successes and positive qualities, he possessed significant aspects of low self-esteem and was very insecure. He refused to face up to his fundamental fears of rejection and abandonment, and no amount of money from work or gambling could remedy his fears. By the time he sought counseling, he had dug a huge hole and was standing in it. He was lonely, ashamed and without purpose, or a ton of money. Although he faced emotional and financial ruin, he could have accepted his mistakes, forgiven himself and bounced back over an extended period of constructive behavior patterns. His friends, including Carl, family and coworkers would have supported him. However, he failed to see the potential strength he could have drawn from of significant others and psychotherapy. Of course, it would have been difficult for him to suck up his pride and "face the music." He would have to unveil his secret life which would have been terribly humbling. Unfortunately, Zane's took the other road and decided to commit the ultimate act of avoidance, suicide. His killed himself while alone in his own home, the way he lived a good part of his life, severely disconnected and suffering. There was no note and no goodbyes. He no longer needed to avoid unpleasant thoughts and feelings. Memories of his father's abandonment and painful comparisons of his life to Carl's no longer had to be endured. The truth is Zane quit primarily on himself and secondarily on his family, similar in process to how his dad quit on him. Ultimately, he became caught in a vicious cycle of self-destruction because he failed to accept his past and what he needed to do in the present. In the end, his escapist strategies failed and he hurt others in the process.

Zane's lack of acceptance of Self was Entitled, Grandiose and Self-Centered. Emotional deprivation aided perceptions of entitlement to the advantages and privileges he saw Carl enjoy. He was Grandiose enough to think he could fast track his way to wealth and Self-Centered enough to "borrow" money from family and friends to gamble with. What would make him think he could beat the odds set by the gambling establishments? These flawed perspectives bled over into lack of acceptance with Others in terms of how controlling he was in hiding the truth of his misperceptions and gambling habit, even with his therapist. Also, he showed his Distrustful side which, at the same time, was Impractical. Why go to a therapist and not be forthcoming with the truth? Finally, pertaining to Life aspects, non-acceptance was exemplified in his Rigid and Simplistic notions that wealth would lead to happiness and security. How could he realistically think that he could feel good about himself and his life while lying to himself and others, living with secrets, gambling, and taking short-cuts to feeling satisfied? His sole purpose for living had become the pursuit of wealth at any cost. As a result, he became divorced from the things and people that could have led to contentment; family, friends, hobbies and work. He demonstrated a Nonreciprocal approach to Life in the sense that he was expecting to get a lot more out of living than he was putting in. He wasn't willing to put much effort into family, work and other fundamental domains of life but was dissatisfied with how he felt about living. Eventually, because he got what he deserved (so to speak), suicide became a rational choice. In reality it was just another form of avoidance, his ultimate and final one. It was yet another action he committed secretly and to avoid further shame and embarrassment. Numerous therapeutic strategies were not enough to stem the tide of his self-destruction. Unfortunately, he engaged in therapy briefly and put minimal effort into a process that could have been successful, with sufficient and persistent effort.

Acceptance Focused Cases

Self

Elena struggled with self-esteem and other-related psychological problems throughout most of her life. She was the eldest of two children, raised by an alcoholic mom and affectionate but mostly absent dad. She came in for counseling in her 50s, married for over 30 years. They had adult children who lived independently and were doing well.

Elena came into therapy complaining of unhappiness and psychological testing suggested depression and anxiety were primary problem areas. In terms of history, she stated always feeling; "odd and different from other kids." She mentioned a long-term battle of her weight and low self-esteem, as well as being a worrier and avoiding of intimacy with her husband for the at least the previous seven years.

Elena had a very successful career and was getting ready to retire in a few years. She looked back at her career with senses of integrity and distinction. However, she acknowledged feeling lonely, scared and confused. She wanted some help and support with getting more direction in her life. As counseling progressed, it became evident that her self-esteem and relationship problems were inextricable and drove her into counseling. Elena was emotionally deprived at home as a young girl and adolescent, and married a decent man but he tended to perpetuate these trends. Predictably, getting married did not spontaneously fill her voids for affection, nurturance and love. Unfortunately, her husband developed chronic medical problems which exacerbated their marital difficulties. He could no longer work and she felt trapped by her conscience. How could she even think about deserting him now? Given her value system, separating from and divorcing him would not help her feel better about herself. Moreover, although unsatisfactory in many respects, she would be giving up the most consistent long-term love of her adult life. At this point, you probably anticipate there is much more the story, and you'd be right!

Elena had been dealing with the above stated issues for some time. Thus, it is unlikely they alone would have driven her into therapy. So, what did? As one might expect, it was an extramarital relationship. Vulnerable to a man who paid special attention to her, she allowed herself to become involved with a coworker. As it turned out, an intimate relationship with him had been going on for about a decade, beginning as a friendship. Although initially a boost to Elena's ego, their involvement gradually lowered her self-esteem and created a long-term bout with depression. She never saw herself as the "other woman." She didn't go looking for another man, especially one who was married. However, she did respond to an overture made by him which parlayed into a sexual relationship she was intensely ambivalent about. Since that time, she had been walking a tightrope and not content with herself. Time with the "other man" helped distract her from marital dissatisfaction and gave her some happy moments but not a sense of peace. Involvement with him was incongruent with her values and commitment to her husband. She felt guilty and anxious when with the "other man" and sad when apart. Gradually, she came to see that her extramarital relationship had stagnated. Unless both ended their marriage and they became a genuine couple, which neither seemed ready or willing to do, their relationship had little opportunity to grow. They didn't spend holidays and vacations together and their friends and families were unaware of the extent of their relationship. How realistic was their relationship? Was there any real purpose to it?

During counseling, Elena was able to look more critically at both her marriage and the extramarital relationship. As sessions progressed, she came to see how she let the "other man" dominate and control when and where they met and for how long. Also, she came to realize she was the giver and he the taker in the relationship. Her gifts, thoughtfulness and sensitivities far outweighed what she received in these regards. She avoided seeing how one-sided the relationship was and came to understand that this is common amongst people who suffered emotional deprivation as a child and/or adolescent. She was accustomed to working excessively hard for attention, approval and love, even when unreciprocated. Elena had learned to tolerate feeling she wasn't "good enough" for others and, when things didn't go well, was inclined to quickly capitulate, self-blame and/ or give into others' wants and needs. As she became more honest with herself and assertive with her infidel, their relationship began to deteriorate. Her expectations and requests for a more reciprocal relationship were not met with cooperation, negotiation, compromise and sensitivity. Elena's willingness to stop avoiding the truth about the relationship helped her see that they were not the special couple she thought. She became aware of her tendency to accept less than she felt she deserved in relationships, due to her history of emotional deprivation. She became determined to stop this merry-go-round. Ultimately, they both backed off. This was difficult because the relationship had become a "bad habit" and escape from her marital unhappiness. However, after ending the affair, Elena felt less anxious and guilty. Moreover, her integrity and self-respect increased, as well as motivation to become more involved with her husband, friends and hobbies. Although Elena's efforts in the marriage were still not as strong as she wished, she was able to significantly revitalize it.

Elena's readiness to confront the realities of her life allowed for a reawakening. She saw her life story much more clearly now and was determined to not waste her energy and time in similar ways. She finally accepted herself and her imperfections. She also accepted her husband and marriage as "good enough." It wasn't what Elena wanted or dreamed of but she knew she couldn't leave him because it was not in her personality make-up to do so.

There wasn't a simple how-to-approach for Elena to enhance her self-esteem. Essentially, she needed to develop insight into the dynamics underlying her behavior patterns and become more assertive in ways consistent with her values. At the same time, she needed to surround herself with more constructive and positive people. These changes were made possible because she was able to stop avoiding some basic truths. Escaping from the misery of her marriage through involvement with a married man neither provided a solution nor was congruent with her ethics. Her extramarital involvement gave her some short-term pleasures but with huge costs. Elena lost herself for about a decade with the "other man" while lowering her self-esteem and integrity to boot. Fortunately, she found herself before it was too late. By changing course, she not only regained what she lost, she was able increase her marital satisfaction, assertiveness, insight, closeness with friends and self-respect.

With respect to Self, Elena had become Self-Debasing. She didn't accept herself and the person she was during the extramarital affair. She was also Unforgiving with herself due to the degree and length of time or her involvement with the other man, along with how she acted in opposition to her core personality. Clearly, she needed to stop acting in ways diametrically opposed to her values, forgive herself for past transgressions she could not erase, and become less self-critical. She also needed to accept the Naïve and Impractical ways she chose to handle her marital and life unhappiness. Could the extra-marital relationship be expected to give her contentment in the long run? Did she really believe she could leave her husband, particularly with a situation like the one she secretly contrived? Not only were they "friends and colleagues" in a small town but what kind of integrity did he show (like her) with the affair? Is this really the foundation for an intimate long term relationship? All they really knew as a couple were stolen moments with one another. Did they really know one another? In retrospect she came to accept that she avoided dealing with her core issues and chose to play in Disneyland for quite a few years. However, Disney proved to be a place of diminishing returns. Over time, the emotional costs far outweighed the joys of play time. Finally, she was capable of accepting that she wasn't Helpless and could make more constructive decisions to counteract a Meaningless existence. Taking more positive control over her social and emotional life helped reduce her Pessimistic and Self-Debasing orientations. ACT-like approaches, self-esteem building, assertiveness training and value clarification exercises were quite beneficial for Elena. She stayed in therapy long enough to make desired changes, although she came back periodically and briefly for "booster treatments" which reinforced what she learned previously in therapy.

Others

Joseph entered therapy stating that his main problem involved an inability to express emotions to others, particularly those most significant in his life. This young man was a college graduate and worked full-time. He liked his professional job and but couldn't see himself performing it for the rest of his life. Joseph recently broke-up with his long-time girlfriend which also was a precipitating factor to initiating psychotherapy. He'd been on Adderall for a few years to treat attention deficit disorder symptoms. It should be pointed out that it wasn't clear he ever suffered from such a disorder per se. His attentional difficulties may have been due to anxiety, immaturity and/or personality disturbance. Also, he attended gamblers anonymous for a past problem associated with losing a good deal of money at casinos.

Joseph reported a fairly solid relationship with his father who he described as strict growing up but now passive and helpful. He characterized his mom as sweet, loving and supportive. However, he also stated she was a recovering alcoholic with whom he had little contact. He has three step-siblings, one of whom he is relatively close to but lives far away.

Due to the dysfunctional nature of his upbringing, Joseph grew up rather shy. He remembers being anxious as long as he can remember. He was part of a reconstituted family wherein some of the family members were psychologically unstable. His self-concept tended to be fragile, although he was a smart, attractive and responsible young man. He adapted by laying low and trying to stay out of controversy at home and school. As a result, he bottled up a lot of feelings and failed to learn how to assert himself properly and consistently. By inhibiting his self-expression, he also deprived himself of important social interactions and feedback that could have provided him with knowledge as to how others saw and felt about him.

Around the time he graduated from college, Joseph met a woman a few years younger. She was intelligent and attractive but also came from a broken family with many dysfunctions. Unlike Joseph, she was outspoken and accustomed to getting what she wanted from her parents. Her self-esteem seemed somewhat inflated and she could get easily frustrated and moody when she didn't get her way. This was the first serious long-term relationship for both. Unfortunately, they were quite immature and lacked a roadmap for how to have an intimate, live-in relationship. Moreover, they didn't realize the poor interpersonal chemistry of their personalities. His girlfriend had a strong sense of entitlement and tended to get critical with Joseph when her expectations were not met. Joseph attempted to adapt as he did during childhood and adolescence by shutting down and not expressing his feelings. Eventually though, he would get hostile and/or withdraw from their environment when his resentment built to a critical level, followed by an apology and then retreat to square one until the vicious cycle repeated.

Predictably, over a period of several years their conflicts and fights reduced their intimacy significantly and they both developed a sense that the relationship would not last. Along the way, Joseph developed a gambling problem and large debt. This was his escape from painful realities, including the fading prospects of their relationship of more than five years. His girlfriend previously entered psychotherapy and he believed it was his turn to do so. He came in to therapy highly motivated to become more aware of his underlying problems and how he could be more productive and content.

Therapy provided Joseph the forum to finally express himself without fear of recrimination. He laid everything out on the table and was able to get insight into how all the pieces of the puzzle came together. It didn't take long for him to decide that he needed to cut off occasional but distracting and purposeless communication with his ex-girlfriend. He not only stopped gambling but he was paying off his debts on a consistent basis. Soon, he would be debt free. He became more open with friends and family and expressed that he really enjoyed his counseling sessions because they were designed strictly for him. He could spend an hour fully focused on his own wants and needs for a change while getting an objective point of view from someone he trusted to keep things confidential. He learned that trying to live up to the expectations others have of him is a choice. He came to the realization that he needed to live up to his own expectations, first and foremost. He accepted that we can only please some people some of the time. Also, he came to accept that is okay for him to be self-interested, as long as he isn't trying to hurt others. It is human nature for us to look out for ourselves and that doesn't make us selfish. It just makes us human. But more importantly perhaps, he learned how to express himself more assertively, as opposed to keeping his feelings and thoughts hidden and suppressed.

These positive and significant changes were made possible because Joseph was willing to face his fears of rejection, abandonment and disapproval. He finally acknowledged that he could not be content and have positive relationships without changing. He was ready, willing and able to shed his self-defeating coping styles and face his deficiencies head on. Of course Joseph, like the rest of us, is not guaranteed a happy and fulfilling life. However, he has a much better chance of securing that type of future now that he is on a more realistic and self-determined course. When therapy was terminated his therapist told him "no news is good news," and he agreed to call if he needed additional sessions. Since his therapist has not heard from him for more than three years, it appears that he is doing fine.

Joseph's Other-related acceptance limitations were primarily associated with being Alienating (passive-aggressive), Controlling, Distrustful and Unemotional (cold). These postures made it virtually impossible for him to develop an intimate relationship over the long haul, particularly someone with acceptance-related deficiencies of their own. As he became less self-centered, he was able to look at others more accurately and at his relationships with greater insight and objectivity. Becoming less Distrustful and Alienating allowed him to be more open and spontaneous while leading to more positive social interactions, as well as more productivity and creativity at work. These changes, in turn, allowed him to be more affectionate and less controlling. A combination of assertiveness training, psychodynamic (childhood/adolescent-related) insight, values clarification, motivational interviewing, self-concept building, and ACT approaches proved quite helpful in getting him on the right track.

Life

Let's face it, parenting is a tough job. It has been called a "labor of love." Sooner, rather than later, we have to make some difficult decisions as parents. Certainly, our parental decisions tend to get more serious as kids get older and, to make matters more complex, we may not agree with our partner on how to react to various situations. It's on-the-job training and can quickly get very personal and emotional. Moreover, to complicate matters further, family members, friends, teachers, and others may weigh in with their opinions, solicited or not. Like marriage and other important roles in life, there are some basic rules of thumb to follow but no real guidebook to tell us what to do with the myriad of situations that will inevitably arise. It is up to each parent to develop their own guidelines along with a certain amount of flexibility and creativity while, at the same time, maintaining adherence to their value system. Parents need to trust that, as long as they are well intentioned and love and respect their children, they will simultaneously grow as a parent alongside their kids.

Walter and Fran met in their 20s and experienced fairly uneventful upbringings. Both came from traditional, hard-working families that were "normally dysfunctional." As they grew into adulthood, like many of their peers, they aspired to the American Dream. They wanted a home, children and satisfying marital/family life. Despite Walter's periods of alcohol abuse, they progressed along these roads quite well. Eventually, they had two children, a nice home in a two career family. Along the way, Walter gave up alcohol with the realization that he could not drink socially/moderately. Things in his life seemed to be on track. However, they started seeing some troubling signs in their eldest, Fred, in the latter part of elementary school.

Fred, a large and physical boy for his age, started to show signs of oppositional defiance and tirades when he didn't get his way. For quite some time, they attributed his inappropriate behaviors to just being a phase he was going through. However, during adolescence, problems became obvious in environments outside the home, such as school and neighborhood. He displayed problems with truancy, poor grades, rebelliousness with authority, and lack of any stable friendship with peers. Although very concerned, Walter and Fran continued their avoidance of the reality of his developing personality traits and refused to get professional help. In retrospect, they can see that they let Fred take control of their family. The daily attention and concerns of the family became centered on Fred's problems, moods and behaviors. What destructive, legal or embarrassing thing would he do next?

Not unexpectedly, abuse of drugs and alcohol became the next step in his digressive states of narcissistic and antisocial behavior patterns. They could no longer attribute Fred's lack of contrition, empathy and guilt to his young age. It was becoming increasingly apparent that Fred was developing an antisocial personality disorder, although they would not see or admit to that until more than a decade later. He regularly took advantage of people without any indication of guilt or remorse which are hallmark signs of this type of disorder. Walter and Fran became enablers early in the process of Fred's development and continued along this vein for far too long. They intervened on Fred's behalf with school teachers and administrators, police officers, magistrates, neighbors, social workers and lawyers. Even with all of their assistance, he failed to graduate from high school and was involved in many legal entanglements. They hired more than 10 lawyers to help minimize or get him out of legal charges, and Walter even flew 3000 miles on one occasion to get Fred out of a drunken state in a motel where he owed a lot of money. Amazingly, although he went to several rehabs and was on probation several times, Walter and Fran managed to keep Fred out of jail. As he grew into his mid to late 20s, Walter and Fran could no longer avoid the reality that Fred had deep psychological problems. They had another child, already in early 20s, who graduated from college and showed expected developmental trends. So, they knew that Fred's problems could not be entirely attributed to their parenting styles. Fred never held a job for more than a week and, although he fathered a child, lost visitation because he failed to pay child support. Of course, it is difficult to pay child support when you don't have a job. When Walter and Fran wouldn't give in to his demands for money or alcohol, he would trash their house, intimidate and bully them or sell his sibling's property to get drugs. It was at this point that Walter and Fran started seeing a psychologist. Their many efforts to get Fred to take psychiatric medication and/or engage in psychotherapy failed. Finally, they were accepting that they needed support and a better understanding of how to deal with Fred and the negative contagion he regularly created. While in therapy, Walter and Fran were able to admit they were burnt out from all the years of stress and problems Fred caused, along with the responsibility they felt for Fred's transgressions. At the same time, they were able to admit that they had neglected their daughter who eventually came in for some family therapy. Clearly, the squeaky wheel received the abundance of grease for quite some time. Fred's sibling had quietly become a mature adult despite being largely ignored because of the constant attention to her brother's whirlwinds. However, the non-squeaky wheel was showing some ill effects of this disequilibrium, including some brooding resentments and feelings of emotional deprivation. As a result, some individual counseling was recommended which proved quite effective for her and led to Walter and Fran feel quite relieved. It also helped family communication patterns which had become dysfunctional in response to the stress imposed by Fred's personality.

At this point, Fred was routinely drinking himself into dangerous blood levels of .30 or more. He was comatose on a number of occasions and was rushed to the hospital for emergency treatment of alcohol toxicity. He actually took some pride in breaking his previous record of alcohol percentage when that occurred. He lost his driver's license due to a DUI but that didn't stop him from driving. He had no means of supporting himself independently and, when occasionally asked to leave the house, refused to do so or broke back into it to get what he desired. Things had gotten to a point where Walter and Fran were afraid to confront his anger, embarrassed to report Fred to authorities, and fearful he might kill himself, accidentally or otherwise. Incredibly, they hoped he would go to jail because they felt he would be more secure there and might respond positively to the punishment and boundaries imposed. Moreover, they wanted some relief from the continuous havoc he created in their lives. Admittedly, they failed to consistently assert themselves over the years and follow through with reasonable expectations and guidelines, as well as sanctions on his behavior. As a result, Fred believed he had them over a barrel emotionally and had no compunction against using psychological leverage (i.e., the suicide card) with them. Finally, Walter and Fran got their wish. Fred drove through a police barricade with an unregistered gun in the car and without a license. He led the police on a long chase and was arrested in another State. Although Walter and Fran got him another lawyer, after telling him they wouldn't do so again, they could not protect him from jail this time. Through their lawyer and court advocate, they made sure that the Judge knew about his history and his need for long-term rehabilitation. The Court was ready to go light on him until they heard from Walter and Fran. After more than a year of incarceration in prison, Fred was put into a long-term work-release program. In the meantime, they helped him get social security disability and sold a second home they didn't want him to live in because they knew he would destroy it. They were set on the notion that he could not return to their home and that he needed to live independently. They understood that they had the right and responsibility to stop enabling their almost 30-year-old son. They seemed psychologically ready to stop taking responsibility for their son's problems. They refused to let Fred's actions contaminate their close but tenuous relationship with their grandchild. They spent a lot of time, energy and money fighting for grandparents' visitation rights, as well as helping out with clothes, gifts, babysitting, etc. They had no intention of risking what they fought so hard for by letting Fred come back into their home. They were afraid that this would give fodder to their grandchild's mother who had legally fought them for visitation. Gradually, they accepted the realities of what could happen with their son. They became more realistic about his Antisocial Personality, alcoholism and prognosis. They were no longer surprised when he showed antisocial behavior patterns. Even with extreme patterns of enabling on their part, Fred almost died on several occasions, never graduated from high school, spent time in prison, failed to give child-support, had no friends, never kept a job, and refused therapeutic support to change his behavior patterns. For whatever set of reasons, he was nothing like his sibling with whom he had no relationship. These were painful realities that could no longer be avoided or denied.

Slowly, Walter and Fran were accepting that their "little boy" would likely never turn out to be the man they imagined. Along with these acceptances, they were able to focus on their own lives and what they could control directly, as opposed to what was outside of their purview. This included more attention and support for their daughter who flourished with these changes. Upon graduation, she got a professional position and nice place to live. Unlike her older brother, she established an independent and responsible lifestyle. In addition, they found their physical and mental health lives improved. These aspects had been ignored for many years and, although they could not make up for lost time, they were able to focus on the "here and now" for a change. This proved to be invigorating and truly a time for renewal. They still have problems with Fred but don't get entangled the way they used to. Predictably, he has changed minimally but no longer manipulates and controls them as he once did. A scenario that helped make some important points with them is outlined below.

> There is a story about a young man who, while hiking in the mountains one day, came across a listless snake. After observing the snake for a few minutes, he came to see that it was dying. So, he decided to ask the snake if this were true. In response the snake weakly replied; "Yes, it's too cold up here." In response, the young man said; "Mr. Snake I will walk down to the valley where it is warmer with you under my coat against my body to help you survive. I will do this if you promise to not bite me. Do you?" The snake replied: "Of course, I promise to not hurt you. That is the least I could do considering you are trying to save my life." The snake was then placed inside the young man's coat and they went down the mountain. Upon decent, the young man could feel the snake begin to move around against his body. When they got to the bottom of the mountain, he reached in and pulled the snake out. The snake proceeded to bite his hand. Surprised, the young man said: "Mr. Snake I cannot believe you bit me. You promised not to because I was willing to try to save your life." Mr. Snake retorted simply with; "What did you expect from a snake?" This story may remind some of the classic book Animal Farm which portrays many different animals on a farm who

represent various kinds of personality types (e.g., pig, fox, snake, sheep, chicken, wolf). Certainly, people can and do change more than animals who are driven largely by instincts. However, the best prediction of a person's future behavior is their past behavior, unless we have good reason to believe they have changed. Trusting someone's promise, apology or word when it hasn't been a consistent theme in their personality functioning can lead to the kind of disbelief described in this story (i.e., "I can't believe you bit me").Why can't you? Isn't that behavior consistent with what you should have expected? Have you been prey to this kind of thinking before where you showed a failure to accept the reality of your past history with someone? If so, with whom did it occur and under what kind of circumstances? Do you see any themes here that apply to your life? If so, do you want to change them and how would you go about doing so?

Walter and Fran mainly shared difficulties accepting Life on its own terms. It took them well over two decades to accept their son's underlying core issues and his recalcitrant nature. They continually returned to Disneyland thinking, despite overwhelming evidence to the contrary. Decades of experiences clearly showed that their approaches were failing and there was only one person who could resolve the issues at hand, Fred. It was extremely hard for them to accept that the net result of their efforts was like throwing good will, effort and investment into an ocean. In the business world the adage is "don't throw good money after bad." In this case they threw good effort and resources after bad. Certainly, it is a more emotional situation when it is our offspring we're dealing with. However, their situation had become like a bad dream that just kept recurring. The foundations of their acceptance limitations were Noncreative, Simplistic and Rigid coping styles to Fred's problems. Their brains continually told them there must be some kind of fix or remedy. However many problems, particularly involving unwilling others, are not solvable. They became mired in a vicious cycle of enabling their son's narcissistic and sociopathic lifestyle while engaging in Impractical coping strategies. As a consequence, they helped support Fred' self-defeating and self-destructive behavior patterns while creating additional frustration and stress for themselves, and failing to place responsibilities squarely on Fred. Fred needed to live with the consequences of his actions and lack thereof. The more responsibility his parents took on for Fred's life, the less motivated he was to act responsibly. They needed to accept that there were no "Why" answers to how he became this way. They needed to focus on "What-if anything" could be done effectively about his problematic life. They informed the author some time ago that they believe they have learned all they could from therapy and finally agree on courses of action which give them a sense of peace. They did not specify precisely what that meant but it was made clear their decision was mutually agreed upon. They had come to accept that there is no solution or fix to their psychological issues with Fred and that they alone have to live with the consequences of their choices. They were finally willing to take independent and creative paths to decision making and live with the consequences, knowing the results are uncertain and could very well be quite negative. It no longer makes sense for them to "grind" over issues while not taking a decisive approach to their longstanding issues with Fred. They have accepted there are no "right" answers, only coping styles and perspectives appropriate for them. They finally understand that they could choose to beat themselves and one another up, no matter what decisions are made. They had become stuck in a vicious cycle of responses to Fred's actions that simply did not work. They needed to decide whether to stay on the same unproductive courses of action or try something new (and not enabling). They knew they could not avoid taking risks. It was a risk (and choice) to do nothing and stick with their same failed approaches; just as it would be a risk to place responsibility on their son and stop bailing him out and enabling him. In the end, they were able to end therapy and stand on their own with a huge dilemma, together in their deep psychological conflict, navigating uncharted emotional waters.

Self/Others

A late middle-aged woman, Marion, came into therapy with a main complaint of: "depression, anxiety and endless worry." When asked to explain the reasons for her complaints, she retorted with "life." Marion possessed no formal history of treatment for her psychological problems. She reported no medical difficulties, although she was distressed about being approximately 70 pounds overweight. She was never gainfully employed and referred to herself as a housewife. She and her only husband of 27 years had three offspring. One of their children has exceptional developmental problems and will never be capable of living independently.

Marion described a poor relationship with her in-laws and a sister who has serious mental health problems and an extensive history of psychiatric interventions. Marion admits that she and her mother used food like a compulsive abuser of drugs, causing her to be significantly overweight for a good part of her life. Ultimately, her mother developed pancreatitis and died in Marion's presence. Her dad excessively consumed cigarettes and alcohol and died at a relatively young age. It is easy to see how Marion learned some of her self-defeating coping styles.

Marion met her husband at a relatively young age and they got married after a short interlude. She described him as: "sweet, caring, hard-working, and compassionate." He successfully developed a family business and routinely put in long hours while remaining available to his created family. He made most of the significant decisions for the family while Marion supported him and the children in the role of a traditional caregiver.

A pivotal factor in Marion's life has been the developmental disabilities of her youngest child. Due to his severe disabilities, he has usurped an enormous amount of time, effort and resources. The person most affected, at least directly, is Marion. Caring for him has essentially precluded her from having a normal amount of time and opportunity to develop in a variety of ways. His special needs have exacerbated her underlying predisposition toward being self-sacrificing and co-dependent. As a result, she went through almost two decades of living a somewhat constricted and unfulfilling life. Marion readily admits that she rarely did anything truly independent, so she never really individuated herself. She struggled with surprise when asked about her hobbies. After long hesitation, she embarrassingly admitted she had none. Basically, she went along with what was deemed in the best interest of the family members while putting her wants and needs in the backseat. Concurrently, she tolerated a good deal of disrespect and passive aggressiveness from her mother and sister in-laws. For example, Marion had difficulty saying no to her mentally compromised and manipulative sister which, by her own admission, served to enable her to continue to treat her inappropriately.

It's not clear whether Marion always had low self-esteem or developed it during adulthood. At any rate, it became a major stumbling block to overcome. She realized that her poor self-concept made it difficult to assert herself and helped lead to and reinforce overeating. She readily envisioned that it was easy to use food as a substitute for other pleasures, and as a way to cope with her suppressed anger in relation to her mother-in-law and sister-in-law. Although her marriage was strong for the most part, their intimacy life was affected by her lack of self-esteem and weight gain. She didn't feel sensuous or attractive and admitted she didn't wear shorts for over 15 years because of her self-consciousness over body image. Marion was approaching an empty nest syndrome which also put internal pressure on her. She felt her marriage was slowly deteriorating and also voiced concern about how her two adult children had been affected by her lack of assertiveness, in-law problems, and their sibling's disability. At her core, she couldn't shake the fear of fading purposes, as nothing made Marion want to get up in the morning with a sense of vitality and appreciation for life.

Marion entered into individual psychotherapy with openness to self-evaluation and willingness to change. She didn't know what or how to change but was eager to learn. She was in a great deal psychological pain and wanted it to stop. She was open to gaining insight regardless of the dynamics underlying her thought and behavior patterns which generally pointed toward avoidance of individuality and independence. She wasn't defensive about how she avoided asserting herself with family members and bottled up feelings, particularly anger, followed by efforts to eat it away. Therapy proceeded along the lines of confronting her tendencies to avoid any type of negative interaction with others. She had become extremely deferent, even in response to being ignored or condescended to. At times, she could recall even having difficulty asserting herself with extended family when they said negative things about her children. In effect, she had become like a rug that others could walk on.

During the early stages of therapy, Marion joined a gym and began exercising routinely. She found a facility where she felt comfortable and the owner became a kind of trainer and life coach. She started watching what she ate and became more assertive with family, friends and acquaintances. Although it may sound somewhat unbelievable, she began to develop goals for herself for the first time. She even skied down bunny slopes to the amazement of her family and wore shorts at a pool party. She was losing weight and feeling better about herself. Others gave her a good deal of approval, although a few women became inappropriately competitive and passive aggressive with her. These apparently envious reactions were no great shock to her, as she was informed in therapy to expect such reactions from some people. Her husband, on the other hand, was more attentive and positive towards her which she was very pleased about. Her relationships with her three adult children improved too, and she was able to gradually wean therapy visits from once a week to once a month. She persuaded her two oldest children to get into counseling too because she felt they had suffered some side effects from her individual difficulties and dysfunctions. Both benefited greatly from relatively brief therapy. This certainly eased her mind with respect to concerns about their not going down the long and winding road she traveled.

Marion was successful in therapy because she was ready to stop avoiding the issues that blocked her from personal growth. She accepted her need to make changes and the reality that long term patterns are hard to change. Marion learned to stop blaming situations and others for her own internal prohibitions. She learned to turn her focus to what she could control directly, her patterns of thought and action. As important, she learned to accept what she could control and prevent escapes into self-defeating acts. She came to understand that she had developed overly defensive coping patterns over many years. She did whatever she could to avoid disapproval, rejection and shame. In doing so she gave up the development of her identity and any chance at being consistently happy or ultimately content. Frankly put, she barely knew who she was or what she liked at fifty years of age. A scenario that helped her is described below.

> You just arrived at the beach. Imagine that you sit on the sand for a while and "people watch." You observe there are basically four types of people there. First, you notice people who essentially never move from their chair or

81

beach towel, some of whom effectively avoid the sun and are not even wearing bathing attire. Some read and others simply talk or watch others on the beach. Some may eat food they probably brought with them. Clearly, food was more important than sunscreen. These people make you wonder why they even came to the beach. Second, you observe people who are somewhat involved with the beach surroundings. They may build a sandcastle and/or walk up and down the shore. They may supervise their children or get something to eat or drink. They are more likely to be wearing a swimsuit and usually arrive late or leave early. Then, there are those who venture into the water and swim and/or surf waves. However, if the water isn't just the right temperature for swimming or they get dumped by a wave, they are quick to go back to sit on shore. Lastly, there are the "go for it" types. If they get tossed around by a wave, they shake it off and go back out to look for a better ride. Which of these types fits you best? Are you satisfied with this pattern? To the extent that life is kind of like a day at the beach, might you want to change some of these patterns? How might you begin making these changes?

Marion's self-acceptance problems revolved around her Self-Debasing and Hypersensitive penchants. She reacted to others' perceptions and reactions too seriously and strongly and was quick to be critical of herself. As a result, people tended to exploit her which served to reinforce her negative attitudes toward herself and others, as well as induce self-defeating actions (e.g., emotionally driven over eating). Assertiveness training and cognitive therapy helped her to be less Alienating and Reactive (passive-aggressive) which improved her confidence, mood and relationships. In addition, she learned to give up attempts at controlling others while taking charge of her own patterns of thoughts and behaviors which she could control. These changes led to fewer conflicts and oppositional attitudes while stripping some of the leverage she had given to others who knew how to manipulate and "get to her." ACT-related treatment helped her see her feelings and thoughts as just that, feelings and thoughts. When she no longer saw them as reality (e.g., If I feel like a loser that doesn't make me one), she could be more accepting of herself and more open and flexible.

Self/Life

Gabriel grew up in a very dysfunctional family. In particular, he had a very negative relationship with an abusive father. Nevertheless, he developed skills in the construction field beginning a very young age. Eventually, he owned his own successful construction business. Most would describe him as a workaholic who was obsessed with doing his work as close to perfect as possible. Although he was motivated by money to some degree, his primary motivation was the satisfaction he derived from a "job well done" and praise that followed it.

Gabriel met a wonderful young woman who he married, and they began working toward a positive future. Then one day while at work, Gabriel suffered a serious accident which turned his world upside down overnight. He went through a long battle with surgeries and pain management procedures which included many medications. Over the next several years, he took more and stronger medications to cope with this chronic pain condition. His physical limitations with his shoulder and back prevented him from working and induced practical dependence on his wife. For the first time in his life, he couldn't cope by being a workaholic. Gabriel felt stuck at home and had a great deal of time to ruminate about his plight and be self-piteous. At the same time, he became physically dependent on opiates and other medications which, little by little, helped strip him of his humanity. His senses dulled and he essentially laid around the house in a stupor. When his wife came home from work, she typically saw that he did next to nothing during the day, except sleep. Although she tended to be very tolerant and understanding, there were limits to what she could stand. After all, Gabriel wasn't an invalid. Although he was granted Social Security Disability, he was still capable of performing light jobs such as housecleaning, cabinetry work, and small furniture construction. Sometimes he would start small projects and leave them unfinished. Other times, he would try to do things he used to do but should not have attempted, only to quit in frustration. One of the only constants in his life was anger. He was deeply resentful with respect to his losses of identity, purpose, productivity and income. He was not even close to accepting the reality of his present and future prospects and limitations. He preferred to numb himself with tranquilizers and pain medications which gave him a "whatever" attitude. A spiraling down effect went on for a few years until both he and his wife couldn't stand it any longer. Eventually, he became suicidal and landed in an inpatient psychiatric hospital.

His hospitalization became a turning point as, among other things, he met the author there who he saw upon discharge in outpatient psychotherapy. The psychologist initially met with Gabriel and his wife jointly. It was during these visits that she expressed her feelings and admitted to enabling Gabriel's self-defeating coping styles. Although supportive, she had no intention of continuing these postures. He came to see that his lack of positive motivation and displacement of anger on his wife was far from a winning strategy. Increasingly, Gabriel realized he was being faced with a choice; "shape up or ship out."

After about six months in therapy, Gabriel got a part-time job with a home and construction distribution center. He realized he could still be productive in and liked being around people again. Of course, being active helped distract him from negative and self- defeating thoughts, as well as his chronic pain. Moreover, his self-esteem was enhanced by his feelings of productivity and the approval he received for tasks completed at the worksite. After being employed for about a year, he realized there was something else he needed to change. He felt it was necessary to get off the heavy pain medication doses he had been for years in order to feel fully human again. It was painful for him to go through withdrawal from the powerful drugs he had taken for so long but, after doing so, his wife exclaimed in therapy; "I got my husband back." They both knew that he was not the person he was before his accident but he became a new and improved post-accident version. He was no longer the unmotivated, depressed and angry man she had lived with for several years.

Gabriel's successes were due to many factors, not the least of which was his supportive wife. However, the key to his turnaround was his acceptance that, although his life would never be the same post-accident, it could still be worthwhile. He was determined to not let his limitations and pain define him. His capacity to come to key acceptances was aided considerably by ending the use of prescription medications, as well as the value and commitment he placed on his marriage, along with the constructive support he received from his wife.

Once he became willing to face what his new life could be like, he was able to engage in more constructive choices and actions. More positive outcomes followed which helped boost his morale and create additional positive momentum. A scenario that helped Gabriel see things from a more positive perspective follows below.

> Think of times you have been tempted to try on some clothing you are interested in buying. However, once you try them on you don't like the way they look or fit. You are no longer interested in them. Note that it is only after you tried them on that you learned something about your level of interest. If you avoided trying them on, you would probably still believe you wanted them. Isn't that how life often is? We have to try on the shoes to see whether we like them or not. Note also that we need to be ready, willing and able to find out whether the shoes fit or not. Another example of this concept can be represented by thinking about a cave. How can we know what is in a cave without going inside? Of course, there may be risks associated with going into a cave and we would want to be prepared for them. However, there can also be possible rewards. A cave could provide shelter if we need it, possess valuable minerals or aesthetic value, satisfy our curiosity, etc. In any case, the point here is that we won't know what is inside until we enter and explore it. Isn't that a metaphor for our lives? How willing have you been to enter caves recently? If you have been avoiding exploration of new areas, how has this affected learning about your interests, capabilities and personality? Do you want to remain outside the cave or are you ready to explore what is inside? Are you willing to test your potential and what life has to offer now and in the future?

Gabriel's work related injury helped spiral him into a Meaningless existence for the first time in his life. He felt Helpless in getting back to his successful business and allowed himself to fall into persistent states of pessimism, low self-esteem and depression which were accentuated by taking too much pain medication. In short, he became self-piteous and filled with hopelessness and purposelessness. Self-related acceptance issues revolved around feelings and perceptions of being Entitled, inability to accept his physical incapacities and limitations (Perfectionistic), and Self-Centered/Debasing attitudes. These areas of non-acceptance put his marriage in jeopardy which further reduced his self-esteem and increased hopelessness and purposelessness. Fortunately, his marriage was important enough to him for their schisms to serve as a wake-up call. Moreover, his wife was involved sufficiently in his therapy and recovery to give him the support and positive motivation required. She encouraged him while refusing to enable his inappropriate coping styles. Once he got off the enormous amounts of medications he was on to numb himself and justify his incapacities, he could see reality more clearly and get out of his Unemotional states. His new insights allowed him to see the side effects of the pain and psychiatric medications, as well as how he used them as a crutch to avoid realities and stressors. Much of his therapy was motivational in nature. Thus, motivational interviewing and existential counseling were quite effective. He possessed the necessary social and emotional maturity to adapt to a new life. However, he needed a great deal of motivation to reinvent himself and redirect his value systems toward revised goals and purposes. His therapy was mainly ACT-related, as his underlying difficulties revolved mainly around emotionally-related acceptances, as opposed to problem solving or solution based orientations.

Others/Life

Freda, a woman in her sixties, came in for outpatient counseling after having permanently lost vision in one eye. She had been treated with eye drops for some time by an optometrist. Although her symptoms worsened during treatment, her eye doctor did nothing to change the diagnosis and simply prescribed more eye drops. Finally, she went to an internationally renowned eye clinic and was diagnosed with glaucoma. Unfortunately, treatment came too late and she lost sight in one eye. Although she was extremely upset with her eye doctor, she was also upset with herself for failing to stand up to the dogmatic and uncaring ways the doctor treated her. Of course, the significant and debilitating effects of not asserting herself greatly exacerbated her negative feelings, including self-blame.

Freda was already having a lot of difficulty in maintaining her specialty food business while, at the same time, cooking and catering for a wealthy business owner. The loss of vision in one eye significantly compromised her capacity to simultaneously work in two businesses. When she wasn't creating her award-winning specialty food, she helped set up dinners for influential professionals and dignitaries at a local mansion. Prior to losing eyesight in one eye, she had a difficult time fulfilling all of her professional and business activities. After the visual loss, she became overwhelmed with stress and started seeing the author because of increased feelings of anxiety, depression, and hopelessness.

A review of Freda's history revealed she grew up on a huge farm in Virginia with several siblings. They lost their mom at relatively young ages and were raised primarily by their wealthy dad who possessed great stature in the local community. Freda developed into a high achieving and responsible young woman who was determined to blaze her own trail. By young adulthood, she became a professional in the performing arts and eventually had her own school and tour group. Just when she finally reached the top of her game, she sustained a devastating car accident. A driver hit Freda's car and caused her to be hospitalized for many weeks. Thereafter, she went through months of rehabilitation. Even so, she was not able to overcome all of her physical and cognitive impairments. This led to her having to quit her coaching and touring career. Unfortunately, her male attorney let the statute of limitations run out on her auto accident case. She trusted that he filed all of the necessary documents as alleged, but that was not the case.

Nevertheless, Freda was still relatively young, talented and determined to get back in the race. Eventually, she invented her own business which yielded enough income for a small home and separate building where she created foods of her own design. Once again, she earned national recognition in a field. She had been relatively content until she lost a significant amount of eyesight. She was now 60 years of age which already tested the limits of her capacity for work routines. Ultimately, these factors led to the loss of her partnership with the man she catered for. Freda had depended on this additional income and the loss of such cause a great deal of anxiety. She was in jeopardy of losing her business and home now. At this point, she reached out to her father who gave her little more than emotional support. He basically told her that he was confident that she would be fine. Although disappointed and frustrated, she was not shocked by his response. He had previously reneged on a promise to let her build a home on his 300+ acre property on a panoramic section of his estate. However, once he dredged a large section for a pond on the parcel he promised her, he grew fond of it and decided against letting her build on his property. Apparently, he was a Southern Gentleman for the public only.

During counseling, Freda came to understand that the relationship with her father, dysfunctional as it was, set the tone for her relationships with other men who followed and had significant and negative impacts on her life. Initially, it was men who took advantage of her while managing her touring dance company. For example, before an opening night engagement, one of the wealthy and powerful board members gave out scores of tickets to his local friends and colleagues, including those purchased by Freda for her family traveling hundreds of miles to see the show. A few days later he tried to blame the loss of receipts on Freda while another board member suggested Freda should keep her mouth shut or face legal charges! Next, it was the lawyer who failed to file crucial forms after her car accident. Then, it was her eye doctor who she acquiesced to and, finally, the owner of the mansion for which she catered. It wasn't until her father failed to give her needed support and Freda entered psychotherapy that she realized that dad made it all possible. To her dismay, Freda came to accept that, beginning at a very young age, she had learned to become deferent, demure and nonassertive with her father. This style became and in integral part of her personality. Thus, she was particularly vulnerable to being taken advantage of by dominant, successful men. Interestingly, she still referred to her father as "daddy." Although she lived in the Northeast for several decades, apparently she brought the Southern Belle with her. As difficult a reality as this was for her, it was a relief to develop this insight. It was actually emancipating for her to finally get closure on a lifetime of unfinished psychological business.

Now, the road ahead was clear. She saw the need for her to finally stand up for herself in terms of her wants, needs and rights. It wasn't long after that she said no to her father when he wanted to change a trust which required all four siblings to sign off on. As she saw it, he wanted her to blindly trust him even though he already had given a large amount of his business to a son-in law. Subsequently, she learned upon his death that his plan was to also bequeath a large amount of the farm to one of the grandsons, cutting out much of the valuable property previously willed to her and her siblings. She had been the only offspring to decline his request to change the trust. Ironically, she was also the only sibling to nurse her father during the many months his health deteriorated significantly prior to dying. It was clear to Freda that therapy helped her accept the reality of the relationship with her dad and the limitations of what she could still control. As Freda began to take more charge of her life and assert herself with new insights and motivations, her counseling sessions became less frequent. She was capable of focusing energy on her priorities, as opposed to family matters and others she could not control or change directly. She was neither blaming herself nor feeling like a victim. Frieda understood that she naturally inculcated personality weaknesses during childhood and adolescence, prior to being capable of fending off such influences. This was not unusual considering the cultural environment and time in which she grew up. After refocusing her energies, she was able to make some adjustments in her business and devote more energy to it. These changes lead Freda to feel more in control of her life while generating more income. Therefore, she was able to reduce the stress associated with fear of losing her business and home which help lift her out of a long-term state of depression. Prior to ending therapy, she thanked the therapist for taking "one million pounds of weight off my shoulders." The therapist responded by saying the counselors can only show clients the paths they may take and clarify the consequences associated with them. It is the client that must choose which roads to travel and live with the consequences.

To sum up, Freda grew up on a sprawling Virginia farm with a Southern Gentleman type dad who she did not really know. While her mother was alive, she protected her and her siblings from his chauvinistic and narcissistic traits. She moved to the Northeast as a young woman to pursue career aspirations but did not realize how Naïve she was about high status adult males and how vulnerable she could be towards men like her father, charming but superficial and manipulative. As a consequence, she did not realize how prone she was to handling social and business situations in Rigid and Simplistic ways. She was overly trusting and submissive in many important life decisions and paid for it dearly. Eventually, therapy helped her get insight into these dynamics. She was able to accept her vulnerabilities and stop blaming her misfortunes on herself or bad luck. Review of these patterns helped her learn to keep her guard up, especially with certain types of men. After finally standing up to her dad, she gained confidence in her ability to assert herself and was able to accept that we can trust other to "do what is in their best interest." Toward the end of therapy, she showed excellent capability of handling delicate family issues when dad became physically incapacitated while living alone on the farm. She handled him and her siblings extremely well under very sensitive and complicated situations involving his estate, power of attorney and need for physical and psychological care. At the same time, she confronted and adequately dealt with a law suit filed against her by former business partners. She surprised them with her assertiveness and emotional strength, even after they hit her with both barrels legally. The old Freda would have run but they were experiencing the new and improved version of Freda for the first time. It may be harder for old dogs to learn new tricks but the resolve that comes with maturity can more than make up for youth when the old dog is highly motivated. Once again, a combination of traditional (e.g. assertiveness) and contemporary (e.g. ACT) approaches proved to be effective rudders in steering Freda's ship toward the directions right for her. In addition, psychodynamic approaches give her insight into the core issue of her father-daughter relationship.

Self/Others/Life

Rhea is in her mid-20s. She is an attractive, healthy, well-educated woman who has a full-time professional job. She lives in an apartment and, until the past few years, was relatively happy and content.

Rhea was raised in a traditional, intact family and is very close to her one sibling. Her family is essentially conventional and tight knit. Rhea was an excellent student and quite popular. In many ways she could be considered the "girl next door," except that as a teenager, she entered Miss

Teen pageants and competed very successfully. As an adult, she won the crown for her home State.

Rhea met a teenage boy a little older than her in the early stages of high school. After becoming friends, they proceeded to date and eventually became an exclusive couple. Over the next 10 years, they grew closer and developed plans to get married and raise a family. She became very close to his family and believed that her future was pretty much staked out.

Then, one day while driving home from work, her car hit a bad patch of road, spun out and flipped over several times. Because of serious injuries, she had to undergo several surgeries and an extensive rehabilitation. Her car was totaled and she was out of work for many months.

Understandably, it took Rhea some time to adjust to the many changes in her life, including Post-Traumatic Stress Disorder (PTSD) sustained from the car accident. For the first time in her life, Rhea was also dealing with insurance companies, a lawsuit, getting behind in work, and the potential that she would have to have additional surgeries in the future.

As is typical with PTSD, Rhea went through a sustained numb-shock period followed by patterns of withdrawal and avoidance. Initially, nothing seemed to matter much, including her relationship with her fiancé. She had difficulty getting motivated for work, exercising and even stopped going out with friends. When questioned by friends and family about what was wrong, she really didn't have any answers. Temporarily, her PTSD condition and associated difficulties put her in the position of being in Avoider for the first time in her life. Figuratively, she had crawled into a cocoon so she could avoid dealing with any additional stress. Of course, the more she withdrew, the more others in her life clamored for her to be the "old Rhea."

When Rhea's emotions of anger, hurt, depression and self-disgust finally reached a peak, she decided to engage in individual psychotherapy. Unfortunately, with regard to her 10 year relationship, it seems she waited too long. Her long-time boyfriend was too impatient to wait for the old Rhea to reappear. A few weeks after she initiated treatment he stopped seeing her and began a relationship with someone else.

At work Rhea was essentially treading water in the sense that she was just doing the minimum to hold onto her job. Her involvement with friends and family was minimal too because, when not at work, she basically hung out at her apartment alone. This was not her previous modus operandi.

With respect to the psychotherapeutic bottom line, there was much for Rhea to accept. Her life had radically changed and it no longer made sense to her. She lost herself and was struggling to find purpose. In turn, she adapted by engaging in social and emotional withdrawal. This type of avoidant behavior was enhancing her depression, lowering her self-concept, and leading to reduced levels of productivity and creativity. The state she had become mired in was reflected in an email he sent to her therapist (see below).

> I'm starting to feel scared of the world. I've come to an abrupt realization nothing is ever as it seems, people are never who we think they are. People don't know who they are so how can we? I feel like everything is one big conspiracy. I feel like when I'm out in public it is just a circus of people walking around with masks on of who they want to be or think they are or who they don't want to be and people who are unhappy are smiling and laughing. People who are sad are the only people showing true emotion. They don't care how they feel or don't even think about it or just hurting everyone around them. I told you a couple months ago how I love the quote "we don't see things as they are, we see them as we are" and I do love it because it makes perfect sense but its truth scares me even more. This is because, if we are always changing by unexpected good, bad, terrible, whatever events, then things around us will change. We will look at them differently. I am sitting in my apartment right now looking at the table I painted and hate it right now. I don't even want to think for a second that it's pretty because I don't know if it's pretty and I don't care if it's pretty right now because I am in a confused, frustrated state of mind. But, tomorrow I might wake up and feel great and remember how cool it was they found the table and the vision I had for it and think of how beautiful it

was. I hate this! I want to view everything beautiful and love everything. But, how could I if there is always a chance of things changing? I am concerned for myself. It makes me want to live only with myself, forever. I feel like I can never trust anyone or their feelings inside knowing they can always change based off life experiences. Or, what if peoples' feelings are not really what they are feeling or they just show who they ideally want to be? I don't know! Also, what if something dramatic happens in a person's life and they are changed forever? What if, for example, I were to find someone and fall in love or develop a friendship and something terrible happens to them which alters their life and how they feel about me? Or, if something happens to me again and I am changed again and I hurt someone's feelings because of how sad I am but can't help how I feel? I'm so overwhelmed by the unexpected because I know how much it can change me and especially since change is the only constant we have. We know things will always change. It's just the fact of the universe. That's how it works. I don't know what I'm going to do or how to accept that this is the world we live in besides living in solitude and only maybe trusting myself to be me, to myself, for myself. But, I still don't know how I am going to inevitably change and that really scares me because now I feel like am afraid to do anything. If the only solution is to surrender to the status quo of a world of maybe, maybe not, not quite, or to acknowledge the difference between uncertainty and absolute, then I refuse. I cannot conform to this. I feel most comfortable and safe when I'm sleeping. Only in my dreams am I secure. Whether they are beautiful or nightmares of my accident, I am safe only there because I know for certain they are not reality. I can certainly confirm that my dreams are absolutely, unrealistic. And, to me that's the only place I can be assured.

Eventually, Rhea was able to get back to a semblance of her prior self. She understood that she needed to reinvent herself. Prior to the accident, she believed that her life plans and goals were set in stone. Her accident set in motion a multitude of significant changes, not the least of which was the demise of her decade long relationship. During therapy, she was able to see the degree to which she had become co-dependent on her boyfriend. She even admitted that her almost 10 year involvement in pageantry was primarily motivated to please her boyfriend. She felt that by being successful in this endeavor her boyfriend would be more likely to believe that he had the "best of the best," be more satisfied, and less likely to leave her.

Ultimately, Rhea came to the realization that she had some important choices to make. She could continue to avoid changes and remain withdrawn and depressed or could face and work through the difficult developmental tasks that lie ahead. Gradually, as she opened up emotionally with acceptance of where she had been and what she was now facing, she engaged in more social interaction and activities. Although she was tempted to deny a promotion which took her to a major metropolitan area a few hours from home, she understood that her decision was to face her fears and restart or continue to throw in the towel.

Post-accident, she developed a lifestyle that was defensive. She was trying not to lose or be hurt, as opposed to winning and approaching pleasure. In the end, her ability to face the symptoms of her depressive and PTSD conditions is what brought her to new heights. She now understands life often does not turn out the way we expect it to but we can turn what appears to be loss into a win. She has experienced that suffering can bring opportunities for change and growth. A scenario that helped her see things from a different perspective is covered below.

> Imagine it is the last inning of a championship Baseball game. You are playing shortstop and your team leads the game 3-2. The other team has the bases loaded and there are two outs. There is a big crowd in attendance, including your friends and family. One of their best hitters is at the plate. What are you thinking? Are you hoping that your pitcher strikes the batter out so you don't have to

make a play? Do you want the batter to hit the ball to you so you can have a chance to win the game? After all, isn't that what you have spent so much time preparing for? In which scenario do you think you would be more relaxed? In which do you think you would perform best? Which manner of looking at this situation is more likely to facilitate enjoyment? Which is more congruent with avoidance? Which is more consonant with how you have been coping? Can you think of other situations in your life where these dynamics apply? If so, do you want to change them? How would you go about that?

Rhea's life up to her mid-twenties was almost idyllic. She grew up in a close knit family with parents who had a solid marriage. She graduated from college, won numerous beauty pageants, had a long-term relationship with a boyfriend she cared deeply about, and was making great strides toward a successful career. She got an excellent job with an up and coming corporation. She and her boyfriend had plans to get married and start a family. Her boyfriend's sister was her best friend and she got along great with her future in-laws. In retrospect, it seemed too good to be true. Then, while driving along on a country road her life took a completely unexpected turn for the worse within a few seconds. Subsequent to her accident, she developed Major Depression and Post-Traumatic Stress Disorders which were understandable reactions. Shortly thereafter, she developed feelings of Helplessness similar to how she felt when her car was spinning out of control. The numbness associated with the PTSD caused her to be Unemotional with others. Eventually, she became Alienating and Pessimistic which are commonly associated with numb and depressed states of mind. Then, when her boyfriend broke up with her she became Distrustful and Controlling. She blocked herself off from people, even family and friends. She attempted to minimize the possibility of experiencing any more emotional pain. However, in doing so she lowered her life satisfaction while increasing and reinforcing her depression. Her Nonreciprocal style reduced positive experiences, as she was receiving little satisfaction from others or even her own activities and endeavors because she put forth such little effort and was so withdrawn.

Gradually, she became more and more Self-Centered and Self-Debasing as she gained weight, spent too much at home ruminating about her plight and pushed people away. She had slipped into uncharted waters for the first time, an ocean of depression. Fortunately, she had solid support from her family and friends and decided to stick with individual therapy as long as necessary. She completed more than 50 visits before finally coming out of her shell. During one of her last visits, she discussed having a new boyfriend and was back to socializing as she did before. She still had some trouble sleeping but denied fear of driving and depression. A new Rhea had emerged and she liked her! She now has the confidence to handle whatever curves life throws her. She plays to win, not to lose. Even though there are massive uncertainties in life and things can change on a dime, she's fully back in the game,

Resilience with Some Therapeutic Support

Marcus grew up in a traditional family with two siblings. Mom stayed home with the kids and dad worked full-time as a professional. His parents eventually celebrated their golden wedding anniversary and, from all appearances, had the ideal family. Of course, things are often not what they appear. Mom was sweet and caring but also deferent to a fault. Dad was loving and a good provider but, at the same time, rigid, controlling and overprotective, especially with the daughters. Everything seemed to go along in a fairly normal fashion until the oldest daughter was in young adulthood. A rift with Marcus's parents led to her moving away from home and never being heard from again. Marcus was the "fair-haired boy" and his sister's flight from the nest elevated his status even more. His youngest sister idolized him and he could do no wrong in her eyes while she became even more overprotected and entitled via her parents.

Marcus was married twice and had three offspring of his own. He was a very successful professional and is now retired. He was well-liked and known in the community. Admittedly, he lost his way in the first marriage by engaging in a "married but single" lifestyle. He failed to address marital problems and showed lack of full commitment to his created family and values. Inevitably, Marcus's forays caught up with him and he experienced an unusual fall from grace. The favored son was finally humbled and everyone close to him knew it. He struggled for quite a few years to find his identity and positive directions. His journey was complicated by many unexpected hurdles. His youngest son was in a tragic car accident with a friend who died. His father passed away, and his ex-wife committed suicide. Moreover, his sister began experiencing bouts of major depression and personality deterioration, precipitated by job difficulties, relationship breakups and the death of their father.

Marcus's dedication to work and support of his three kids never wavered. However, now single for the first time in decades, he hit the party scene. Marcus was a work hard, play hard kind of guy, so he hit the ground running in this arena. His use of alcohol accelerated and he had little difficulty finding female companionship because he was tall, handsome, confident, articulate and successful.

Understandably, Marcus had a hard time finding a meaningful relationship with his partying strategy. However, he eventually met a remarkable woman who also survived her own set of life altering events and family upheavals. Initially, they hit the social scene in a fast and furious pace. However, as the glitz and glitter of living as if they were in their 20s once again faded, a renewal began. They got married and bought a house of their own. More importantly, they began a spiritual journey together. They regularly attended Church and Marcus' wife volunteered extensive amounts of time to help those in need. Marcus made amends with his children and in-laws and rededicated himself to the values he failed to adhere to during his first marriage. He realized that perceptions of entitlement took him far afield from the person he truly wanted to be. He acted as if having sex, irrespective of the circumstances or type of woman he got involved with, represented some kind of major priority in his life. Ultimately, he found this was an empty form of existence.

Unfortunately, shortly after Marcus got his life back together, his resolve was tested mightily due to the tragic and sudden death of one of his adult children. Not surprisingly, this huge loss catapulted him into grief counseling. He was in a state of severe depression. He had suffered from depression previously but was able to get out of it before it became chronic. He wasn't so sure he would be able to it without support this time. Psychotherapy, along with family support and religiosity, helped Marcus get measures of resignation sufficient for him to gradually work his way out of acute depression. He openly discussed his pain in therapy and with his family members, and then reached out to others who have experienced similar fates. These acts of approach, as opposed to avoidance, helped him heal from the deep wounds inflicted by his son's early demise. He readily acknowledges that he will probably never reach full acceptance with respect this loss. He will always feel a sense of sadness and incompleteness. There will always be something missing in his life. He can say that presently he is in a state of resignation with respect to his son's death. However, he doubts that it is something that he will ever feel okay about. In other words, he can accept the reality of the loss, and speak about his son without breaking down emotionally, as he did previously. However, he does not believe that he will ever get over the sadness and loss associated with not being able to see his son, hear his voice again, follow his development, become closer friends, etc.

Marcus' travels through adult life passages make the author mindful of what Gail Sheehy (1983) called a Pathfinder. Pathfinders are adults who negotiate the travails of adulthood in constructive and creative ways. They do not succumb to major life setbacks with self-defeating patterns. Rather, they remain optimistic and find ways to connect meaningfully with others while revising their purposes and goals in ways that fit their new environments and challenges. Certainly, they do not avoid or retreat from relationships, as they are aware of their need for support, affection and feedback from others, especially when life circumstances change significantly. They come to understand that adulthood is a relatively continuous process of development and requires constructive responses to changes, both external and internal. Non-acceptance of these realities almost assuredly dooms us to an unsatisfying life, at best.

Marcus didn't require formal psychotherapeutic techniques or interventions. He simply wanted someone supportive to speak with confidentially who could listen empathically. He also needed feedback as to whether or not what he was experiencing was natural and expected. He knew there were no solutions to what he was experiencing and that he needed a great deal of time to heal, to the extent possible. He understood the healing process would probably never be complete and that suffering is an inevitable part of life. He avoided blaming anyone, including himself, although he admitted there were things he would do differently if he could turn back the clock. He accepted there were questions he will never get answers to, which is inevitable. Finally, he continued to seek and find support and strength from his wife, family, friends and spiritual network, as well as continue to live his life as meaningfully and purposefully as possible. He acknowledged that is what his deceased son would want.

Resilience *without* Therapeutic Support

Curtis grew up in a lower middle class family during the 1950s and 60s. He had two siblings and hard-working parents who were part of what has been referred to as the Greatest Generation. His parents survived the Great Depression and World War II. They learned to value teamwork, responsibility and independence. Both were scarred by father absence and developed difficulties in expressing emotions. They focused on competitiveness and upward mobility. Curtis and his siblings knew they were loved and supported but received little affection or direct guidance. In retrospect, Curtis understood this style of parenting, including corporal punishment for misbehavior, was common amongst his cohorts.

Curtis developed into an excellent student athlete and was popular during high school. He obtained a job before his older sibling to pay for his own car at 16. He turned out to be quite precocious in many ways which had its advantages and disadvantages, like most things. Along this vein, as a freshman pre-medical student in college, his high school girlfriend became pregnant. It wasn't long before he did the "right thing" and they married. He quickly got a full-time job while continuing his college studies. Needless to say, he couldn't maintain his pre-med classes or college athletics while working full time and supporting a new family.

Curtis proved to be very adaptive and capable of handling an enormous amount of responsibility at a young age. However his wife grew impatient with their new lifestyle and felt trapped. She wanted to be out with her friends and be part of the social scene. Eventually, temptation won out and she sought and gained a divorce from Curtis. This was devastating to him and, for the first time in his life, he became significantly depressed and resorted to occasional use of alcohol to an excessive degree. He didn't get involved in psychotherapy which would have been unusual for that time period. However, he did receive a good deal of support from friends and family which helped him rebound from what he considered his first significant failure.

Curtis eventually gravitated toward positions in the business field, although he had no education or formal training for this type of work. However, he had excellent social skills and was very intelligent. Because he had a daughter to support, he also had strong incentive to be a successful provider. He met an impressive young woman along the way and they eventually married and had children. However, as often happens in life, he had another major setback during young adulthood. He learned that he had a chronic and potentially debilitating medical disease, one he inherited from his father. He had to begin taking medication for this disease in his twenties and knew that it would progressively get worse. Nevertheless, he accepted it and continued to work his way up the corporate ladder. Unfortunately, his second marriage didn't work out but he continued to provide for his children and became one of the top people in his field. In his position as head of global operations for a Fortune 500 company, he traveled all over the world. He was able to do this even while laboring under a chronic disease, taking medications, and having to undergo occasional surgeries. Eventually, he underwent an organ transplant which led to various medical problems associated with the anti-rejection drugs he had to take. Subsequently, he had to undergo two surgeries requiring removal of cancers most likely caused by the anti-rejection medication.

Today, Curtis enjoys retirement and performs some consulting work. He enjoys traveling and spending time with his three adult children, two grandkids and significant other. He experiences a great amount of integrity associated with his accomplishments and relationships. Curtis experiences the contentment that can only come from facing challenges and problems head-on, and the maturation associated with such. He never quit, although there were times he thought about it. Somehow, he despite tough odds, he was always capable of reaching down deep and doing the best he could with what he had, which was plenty.

Certainly, Curtis was aided by observing his parents who were hard-working, competitive and independent. They too were not the type who shied away from challenges or problems. They were hardy people who didn't make excuses, justify mistakes or avoid responsibilities. On the contrary, they sought opportunities and challenges. For example, his mother traveled to China to be with her second husband who flew commercial planes for the Emperor. Tragically, he died in a plane accident and she had to take the slow boat back to the United States with nothing but memories and a few artifacts. Still, it wasn't long before she got out of her mind and into living once again. This led to her meeting Curtis's' dad (to be). Likewise, Curtis's dad was constantly learning new skills. For example, he took home correspondence courses to learn electronics and built a "ham radio" station so he could talk to people all over the world long before the Internet. He also translated his electronic skills into a part time business fixing phonographs, radios, televisions, etc. His dad had a pilot license to fly small planes, hunted, performed all of the mechanical work on the cars and home, and still found the time to coach community baseball teams for many years. At the same time, his mom was a "den mother" for the cub scouts and became the first female president of a local little league baseball organization. She also found the time to garden, become an excellent cook, write advertisements and enter crossword puzzle contents. Among other accomplishments, she was invited to be on a national television program for an advertisement contest she won. She won the grand prize for her entry which was not surprising because she won smaller prizes for "jingles" and crossword puzzles on a fairly regular basis. These are just a few examples of the multitude of things his parents modeled in terms of how to be active, engaged, and open to new experiences and growth oriented. In the end, this background helped Curtis confront and accept the stressors he faced which helped reinforce his confidence to find independent and creative ways to adapt and grow.

Curtis consistently "did it his way" while negotiating down the many and varied crossroads of life. Although he was educated in the biological sciences, he became extremely successful in the business world. He could have coped with the many major setbacks and stressors he faced in other ways; ones involving common self and/or other-destructive patterns like alcohol and drug abuse, gambling compulsions, over-eating or any number of other similar avoidant/escape themes. Recall the case of Zane wherein he self-destructed and hurt others in the process. Curtis' "I did it my way" approach might make us mindful of the following scenario that can be helpful in increasing our ability to find our own creative solutions, as opposed to doing the simple thing in the short run or simply following the crowd.

> Imagine you are in a crowded theatre enjoying a movie. You are engrossed in the film when someone shouts "fire." You don't see the fire but you can spot smoke coming from the floor and ceiling. Suddenly, you hear people yelling and running toward one of the exits. People are pushing and shoving to get out as quickly as possible in hysterical fashion. Do you imagine yourself following the crowd or waiting briefly to stay away from the stampede and see if you want to take a different exit? If you follow the herd so to speak, you may go right toward the fire. Is it possible that waiting a few seconds to make your choice may lead to a more independent and creative one? Is this something that you routinely do (i.e., take the road less traveled)? If not, can you think of times you wished you had? Do you want to work on changing this about yourself? Can you think of any particular areas of your life you want to target for discussion of this topic?

Curtis has lived his life with humility and strength. He hasn't been the type of person who passes himself off as a role model or someone who has all the answers. He has learned to role with the punches that Others and Life have thrown his way with grace, courage and forgiveness. First and foremost, he is a family man with strong spiritual values. Although he was very successful in his career endeavors, his achievements were built on a foundation of family values and ethics, as opposed to working for status, power and acclaim. He was also patient with his career goals, as he was content to earn his way up the career ladder via teamwork, persistence and dedication toward a job well done. He exemplified the importance of doing the right things for the right reasons. As a consequence, Curtis avoided get rich schemes and cutting corners. He took the long persistent route, as opposed to making risky or self-centered decisions he would likely regret down the road. He can look back now at how many hills and mountains he climbed with pride and a deep sense of accomplishment. Above all, he creatively found ways to essentially accept Self, Others and Life, as difficult as that can be for all of us. At the same time, unwavering commitments with his creatively designed goals, purposes and value systems helped him confront the people, places and things that inevitably needed to be dealt with to have a productive and meaningful life.

Chapter Six

Avoidance and Other
Psychological Disorders

It is commonly understood that we acquire most of our skills via positive reinforcement. Certainly praise, approval, attention, money and awards have powerful influences on the development and maintenance of our behavior, particularly adaptive and productive ones. On the other hand, anyone who has worked in the mental health field sees the power of avoidance forces a daily basis. It is become clear to this author that the battle line usually involves helping clients face their anxieties and responsibilities while continuing to move them moving toward constructive action. There's only way to tear down the walls of anxiety and stress and that is to dismantle them piece by piece. Eventually, there is only one way to get over the fear of flying and that means getting our butt on an airplane, whatever that takes.

Unlike adaptive behaviors, maladaptive behaviors are primarily caused and/or perpetuated by negative reinforcement which includes avoidance and escape paradigms. Note that anxiety is associated with avoidance of situations (e.g., imagined rejection, embarrassment, failure) whereas fear is related to getting away from actual objects (e.g., planes, snakes, heights). Both are under the operant conditioning rubric of negative reinforcement. (i.e., relief from anxiety or fear occurs when we avoid or escape from the object of our unpleasant emotion). Without question, the reduction of anxiety and fear via avoidance and escape-related behaviors is an extremely powerful force on behavior. As a result, the use of negative reinforcement is replete in our society because of its effectiveness. Just see what happens you don't pay your bills on time. Clearly, patterns of running from our anxieties and fears will cause our problems to increase, along with our self-doubts. We will begin to question our emotional strength, willpower (self-control in psychological terms) and courage. Furthermore such patterns, like any other repetitive behavior, can become habitual. Finally, the "runner" runs the risk of engaging in response generalization (Watson, 2007). This involves a tendency for the individual to run from similar situations. Examples of this are represented by persons who do not get over their initial fears which they let hang around and fester. As they lose confidence in their ability to handle situations they see others dealing with or they used to, fears tend to spread like a disease. Ultimately, some will develop a chronic state of pervasive anxiety, while others will exhibit symptoms of agoraphobia, obsessive compulsive disorder, or social anxiety disorder. Eventually, most of these people will become depressed because their lives will be rigid and truncated, thus leaving them dissatisfied on a regular basis.

The author has found a shortcut method to get at, or at least close to, the root of the psychological problems of most clients. This involves a simple question along the lines of; "What have you been avoiding?" This question can quickly reduce what otherwise seems to be a nebulous and complicated mess into a general theme of avoidance/escape, including: false assumptions about life, irresponsibility, patterns of running from stressful situations, lack of assertiveness, fear of intimacy, escape (e.g., so-called addictive behaviors), etc.

Consonant with what was pointed out by Glasser (1998), this author has found that most people enter into psychological treatment because of relationship difficulties. Usually, difficulties in relationships or the lack of having an intimate one are the primary reasons individuals seek help. Not surprisingly, relationship problems are frequently associated with avoidance of dealing with the underlying causes of lack of intimacy, conflicts, poor communication, etc. Occasionally, relationship conflicts are secondary issues but much more often there is primary angst over problems with people at work, in-laws, family of origin, children, etc. Loneliness, fears of rejection and abandonment, relationship loss, parent-child and marital conflicts, speech and social anxiety, and other social/relationship issues dominate discussions in psychotherapy. Therefore, it becomes clear that avoidance and escape-related tendencies associated with relationships and social interactions will need to be routinely and comprehensively addressed by therapists.

Although this book has thus far concentrated primarily on the role avoidance plays with chronic depression, the case could be made that it is relevant in similar ways with many other psychological disorders. Chronic depression was highlighted in this book because this author has witnessed it to be so often overlooked and misunderstood, despite the fact that millions of people suffer from this condition. However, although the content (i.e., symptoms) across different types of psychological disorders varies, there is reason to believe that the underlying processes for most (avoidance/escape) do not. Recall the results of the study involving administration of the MCMI with over 1200 outpatients. Note that the personality scale results for individuals scoring significantly on the Major Depression, PTSD and Anxiety Scales were very similar to those found with the Dysthymia Scale (chronic depression). This common theme of avoidance/escape may help explain why co-morbidity rates tend to vary from about 60 to 80%. As pointed out earlier, if a person has one psychological disorder, then it is more than likely they have two or more disorders (Sue et. al., 2013). To put this into perspective, let's assume an individual is diagnosed with an eating disorder. It would not be uncommon for this type of person to be diagnosed also with Persistent Depressive Disorder, a form of substance abuse and Borderline Personality Disorder. Given what we have discussed in this book so far, it seems reasonable to ask whether it is possible that two or more of these disorders have a common theme, namely excessive patterns of avoidance and escape, including inhibitions with respect to accepting important aspects of their life. Consonant with what has been discussed thus far in this book, the answer to this question is a resounding affirmative.

Along this vein, it is been found that anxiety and depressive disorders correlate very highly, so that people with a depressive disorder are likely to be diagnosed with a form of anxiety disorder and vice versa. As a matter of fact, the relationship between these two disorders is so overlapping that some theorists and researchers have argued they form a unitary constellation that can be referred to as a neurotic syndrome (Weinstock et. al., 2006). This finding suggests that there is a common theme or set of themes that runs through both disorders. If so, then it would seem that a parsimonious approach would likely be beneficial. So, rather than viewing and treating them as separate disorders, honing in on common themes which represent underlying core issues may be a more cost effective approach. Certainly, this type of approach should help reduce the possibility that both the client and therapist focus excessively on specific symptoms and "miss the big picture." Also, clients are likely to feel less overwhelmed and "damaged" at the prospect of having to address separate disorders, as opposed to focusing on unifying themes. In addition, they are likely to get enormous amount of relief when they feel that someone finally sees and understands the underlying nature of their psychological problems, not to mention the positive effects of the insights gained by this approach. Eventually, they will be able to more clearly identify the nature of their self-defeating patterns, as well as how to exit the cul-de-sacs they are wasting energy on, so they can enter and travel down thru streets. Discussion of how avoidance and escape patterns are involved with the development of other common psychological disorders, as well as treatment considerations, follows.

Anxiety Disorder

As one might expect, anxiety disorders are usually inextricable with patterns of avoidance/escape. For example, it would be unusual to find a person with social anxiety disorder who is not also diagnosed with avoidant personality disorder or at least shows symptoms of such (Dolan-Sewell et. al., 2001). Moreover, as pointed out earlier, the person with social anxiety disorder will often be depressed. Whether avoidant personality is a primary cause of social anxiety disorder and/or effect of such, how can anyone expect to get over it if they continue to engage in excessive patterns of avoidance and escape? Additionally, it is obvious that people suffering from phobias have difficulty getting past their irrational fears because they continue to use avoidance and escape strategies. Once again, these coping strategies will provide temporary relief but also serve to maintain the phobic disorder.

In recent years, ACT has developed some effective treatment methods for anxiety disorders. From an ACT perspective, rather than envision anxiety as something to tolerate, reduce or manage, it is seen as an inevitable and natural part of living. As with depression, ACT approaches include mindfulness exercises which involve a combination of relaxation and visualization components. Additionally, therapists teach and employ a number of exercises and metaphors to help clients become more accepting, self-aware, motivated/committed, and focused on the here-and-now.

Anxiety disorders are the most common form of diagnosed psychological condition, and the most frequent psychological symptom people report (Sue, et. al., 2013). Not surprisingly, chronic and marked levels of anxiety can run a person down to the point where they develop depression. Moreover, people with high levels of anxiety often avoid important aspects of living which increases the probability that they will suffer from depression. Recall the research findings with the MCMI-II reported in Chapter Two. It was mentioned that people with a significantly elevated Anxiety Scale showed similarly strong relationships with the personality patterns associated with various styles of avoidance, as did those with a significant Dysthymia Scale.

Control issues are generally central with people diagnosed with a form of anxiety disorder. Typically, individuals with anxiety disorders are attempting to control or get rid of anxiety. As humans, it is natural for us to attempt to control or get rid of unpleasant experiences and situations. However, an important distinction should be made here about when control is likely to work versus make things worse. With small matters most of us are able to control our anxiety with simple distractions, such as think about A rather than B. For example, we may be having trouble going to sleep and we tell ourselves to stop thinking about something we're concerned about, and instead, focus on something neutral or pleasant. Or, we may be successful with a simple thought stopping approach consistent with traditional cognitive behavioral therapy (Watson, 2007). This would amount to simply telling ourselves to "stop it" in reference to what we've been thinking. However, what happens when a person is experiencing strong or overwhelming anxiety and associated thoughts? In this type of case it may very well be that trying to control thoughts will backfire and make the situation worse. Powerful thoughts, urges and sensations can be extremely difficult to ignore. So, we may tell ourselves to "not think about X." In doing so, haven't we just brought to mind X? We see a similar dynamic with chronic pain patients. It can be very hard for them to deliberately not focus on their pain. However, when asked about their pain perceptions when they were watching an engrossing movie or favorite sporting event, they typically admit being distracted and feeling less pain. Not only can anxious thoughts increase with attempts to control them, we can lose confidence in our ability to control our thinking when we fail to force ourselves to not think about something. It is kind of like trying to force ourselves to go to sleep. Does that work or is a better strategy to concentrate on relaxing or thinking about something else?

It is generally understood that confronting anxieties and fears will heighten our arousal and desire to avoid. However, behavioral "exposure" assignments are designed to reduce avoidant behaviors, as opposed to avoiding negative internal (emotional) responses. In effect, the client is guided into accepting the discomfort of facing distress while not evaluating how they are progressing based on how they feel. In other words, when we face our anxieties and fears, we are making progress, even if we experience negative emotions. Note that this is very different than how most clients have been perceiving things. They tend to believe they should to be able to get through certain situations without feeling anxiety or fear. This orientation is not only unreasonable but can lead to additional frustration, anxiety, depression, and low self-esteem. At the same time, they are encouraged to see their internal events (feelings) as transient, as opposed to threatening experiences that must be avoided. These orientations help clients defuse (separate) from the ways they had been relating to their difficulties while increasing their willingness to experience the unpleasant feelings that accompany facing internal and external stimuli associated with discomfort and distress.

Substance Abuse Disorders

It is usually easy to get people with substance abuse disorders to admit they have a strong penchant to avoid and/or escape from negative emotional experiences and life situations via the use of some type of psychoactive substance. Understandably, it doesn't take long before they have learned to avoid and escape stress via tranquilizing medication, painkillers, alcohol and/or drugs. The relatively quick and temporary relief received from their psychoactive substances of choice acts as a strong form of negative reinforcement. Of course, once they are psychologically and/or physically dependent on a psychoactive substance, they are also motivated to continue use to avoid withdrawal. More importantly, psychoactive substance abusers often engage in other forms of avoidance/escape (i.e., negative reinforcement), because of the side effects of their primary gain (i.e., relief from anxiety and fear). So, regular users typically engage in other behaviors that fall under the auspices of negative reinforcement (i.e., avoidance/escape). Anyone who works with so-called addicts sees these ramifications on a consistent basis. Examples include alcoholics frequently lying about how much they drank, drug users stealing money to avoid withdrawal symptoms, and abuse of painkillers to induce a zombie-like state for avoidance of responsibility or memories. They even switch drugs via poly-substance abuse to compensate for fluctuations in mood and consciousness states (i.e., take uppers to get more aroused and downers to calm down). Eventually, Avoiders create additional stressors for themselves that increase their desire to use psychoactive substances. Problems associated with irresponsibility, legal entanglements and/or relationship conflicts and alienations inevitably accrue which help maintain the vicious cycle of negative emotional states and substance abuse.

The person wrapped up in this vicious circle obviously confronts a quandary. Briefly put, they need to accept the inevitability of psychological stress and pain they avoided in the short run and unintentionally enhanced in the long term, while simultaneously increasing their commitment to a set of purposes consistent with a coherent set of values and goals. Certainly purposeful action in the service of important values can help them overcome their desire to "use" and not return to their previous patterns of psychoactive substance abuse.

Substance abusers are often reluctant to make commitments because they are afraid they will break them. They need to understand that they are not making an outcome commitment. Rather, they are making a value commitment which could include failure. Therefore, their commitment to abstain from drug or alcohol abuse does not mean they will never use again. Should they fail and relapse, then they can commit to getting back on track soon as possible (Wilson et. al., 2010).

The focus of ACT approaches is that substance abuse is essentially a form of experiential avoidance. Avoidance patterns lead to a loss of flexibility and vitality in users and, as pointed out above, avoidance begets avoidance. Eventually, the user sinks into a meaningless life full of despair. As the user gradually faces their obstacles and difficulties, a life of value emerges. Their pain does not disappear but it is now pain with purpose.

There have been many studies showing the effectiveness of ACT with substance abusers. More interestingly perhaps, there are empirical data demonstrating that experiential avoidance is associated with both the development of addictions and a deterrent to initiating treatment. In other words, is been found that getting "high" tends to be both stimulated by negative private events and used to regulate them (Armeli, et al., 2003).

Interestingly, a large scale study on alcohol and substance abuse was conducted by the National Institute on Alcohol Abuse and Alcoholism (Peele, 2004). More than 42,000 Americans responded to a survey of their lifetime use of psychoactive substances. Of the 4,500 or so who had been dependent on alcohol at some point in their life, only 27% had been engaged in treatment at any point. Of this group, about one-third (9%) were still abusing alcohol. Of those who never had any treatment for their alcohol abuse, only about one-quarter were still diagnosed as an alcohol abuser. Therefore, most individuals who abuse alcohol or become dependent on it never get any treatment for such. Moreover, most people who overcome their substance abuse problem do so without any formal help. These data help demonstrate how important motivation is in effectuating change. Interview and survey responses from this sample showed that people were ready, willing and able to change when their values and priorities shifted to maintaining their employment, keeping their families together, living a longer life, staying out of legal trouble, etc. In other words, they came to understand that there was little chance for them to have a quality life unless they stopped or significantly curtailed psychoactive substance use. Consequently, Peele concluded (p. 46): "These findings square with what we know about change in other areas of life: People change when they want it badly enough and when they feel strong enough to face the challenge, not when they're humiliated or coerced."

Posttraumatic Stress Disorder (PTSD)

Avoidance and escape strategies are central to the maintenance of PTSD. The emotions, thoughts and memories related to traumatic events are not pathological in and of themselves. Rather, it is the extent to which a person will go to avoid or eliminate anxiety and fear that is dysfunctional. Recall the strong relationship between avoidance styles and PTSD reported in Chapter Two. In the ACT model, acceptance and willingness to regain committed actions toward valued goals provide alternatives to continued patterns of avoidance and escape. Trauma survivors are usually living a much more self-restricted life than before they developed PTSD because their new life is dominated by motivation to avoid and escape from thoughts, feelings and memories associated with traumatic experiences.

Avoidance and escape behaviors tend to perpetuate because of three main factors (Varra & Follette, 2004): short- term relief provided by avoidance and escape behaviors, the client fusing with the trauma (e.g., I am emotionally marred forever by this event or series of events), and the mistaken notion that emotional avoidance will work. Getting the client to return to more committed action in line with their value orientations is vital to their recovery. Unfortunately, they frequently have difficulty articulating and envisioning what they desire. They usually spend such a large amount of time and energy on avoidance and escape patterns that they haven't been adequately focused on their future. Also, because they tend to see themselves as "broken," it is difficult for them to imagine themselves as strong enough to obtain long-term important goals. Many PTSD sufferers had no control over being traumatized and used dissociative and avoidance/escape coping mechanisms to minimize their suffering. They need to understand that the coping mechanisms that helped keep them intact during and around the time of their trauma are now lowering their potential to live a purposeful life.

Companion Dysfunction

There is no question that the psychological health of individuals comprising a couple influences the well-being of the couple and vice versa. In other words, poorly functioning individuals tend to cause significant marital dysfunction which, in turn, facilitates more psychological problems with each partner. Unfortunately, in most cases both sources of dysfunction are present. Of course, children often display maladaptive symptoms as a result which causes more stress and dysfunction for the parents. For example, Whisman, Sheldon & Goering (2000) found about that about 70% of psychological disorders (mostly anxiety and depression) were associated with marital/partner conflict and dissatisfaction. Not unexpectedly, the obverse has been found too. That is, individual psychopathology facilitates couples' conflicts and marital dissatisfaction (Fruzzetti, 1996). Put in more basic terms, it is very difficult to be happy and content with our lives if we are not in a mutually satisfying relationship with our partner.

We all need to feel validated and "good enough." At the same time, people who are not balanced psychologically are essentially incapable of maintaining effective, intimate relationships. Ironically, the most "needy" are typically the least capable relationship-wise. Although it is a truism to say that we must love ourselves before we can love anyone else, it seems obvious this is only partially true. We cannot fully love ourselves without some external validation. Imagine how difficult it would be to love yourself if you were the only person in the world or marooned on a faraway island. We are social animals that need positive feedback from others, at least now and then. We cannot and do not love in a vacuum. It is through acceptance by others, as well as our own self-acceptance, that we are psychologically stable and content. Our self-acceptance allows us to turn our attention to our mate when desired or needed, so that we can empathize and understand their perspectives and points of view.

David Schnarch's (1998) conceptual framework fits nicely into what has been exposed in this book. He envisions that at any given moment we all possess a level of what he calls "differentiation." Simply put, differentiation could be thought of as a kind of relationship maturity. Highly differentiated people have an ability to maintain contact and intimacy with their mate without losing their identity, even while going through high degrees of stress and conflict. In essence they are capable of reacting in mature ways to disagreements, rejection, differences, and unexpected blows without engaging in childish behaviors we are all familiar with, including threats, intimidation, tirades, avoidance, escape, blaming, etc. As he points out, our sympathetic nervous system is wired to respond with a flight or fight syndrome when norepinephrine and other biochemical changes alert and mobilize us for survival. Our natural mammalian tendency is to run and/or attack, neither of which promotes healthy relationships. These coping styles may work for the individual in the short run by causing intimidation, appeasement, fear, insecurity, etc., but, in the long run, are almost assuredly counterproductive tactics. Couples cannot grow in their relationship unless non-avoidance and acceptance prevail over more primitive biological responses. Surely, our survival depends on sympathetic responses to truly dangerous situations. However, reacting to our mate as if our very survival is at stake on a routine basis is the path to nowhere but discontent or worse. When we try to change or escape from our mate's behaviors or perspectives through threats, manipulations, control or other negative means, they are likely to rebel, respond similarly, and/ or emotionally have less fun and affection to share with us. On the other hand, acceptance of our mate (assuming their behavior is not way out of bounds), together with assertive communication of our feelings and compromise when feasible, are much more likely to maintain and enhance connectedness and intimacy. Oppositely, both runners and fighters alienate others with their refusal to face issues that are inevitable in marriage and family life, not to mention unexpected chaos and trauma that can befall any one at any time. Runners leave their mate holding the bag so to speak while refusing to communicate or take responsibility and leaving their partner without attention or affection. Often, they are also attempting to impose guilt or gain sympathy instead of facing their own internal prohibitions against changing their behaviors and perspectives. They would rather be "right" than do the right thing. At the same time, they tend to be oblivious to how their running and fighting affects their mate. Who really wants to live with someone who punishes, threatens, attacks or punishes when they don't get what they want, and withdraws or escapes when we do not acquiesce? Clearly this is the road to inhibiting communication, spontaneity, fun, and intimacy, as well as facilitating possible infidelity and exacerbating conflict. Poorly differentiated couples typically have very little to talk about beyond mundane aspects of life. They drift inadvertently into shallow and superficial verbal communication because there are very few "safe" topics to discuss. They have failed to successfully address many of their differences with negotiation, compromise and/or acceptance and tend to avoid the endless and circular arguments that plague their marriage. So, they are now at dinner or in the car and find themselves talking about their kid's activities, weather, friends, etc. while avoiding discussion of future plans and goals, how they feel about one another, their real differences and how they can be better handled, etc. Nonverbal communication is usually as stifled, if not more so, than verbal communication in the marriage. This shows up in almost all cases in the bedroom. Sex tends to become much less frequent and intimate in style. It is probably the most important aspect of nonverbal communication in most marriages. Years of experience performing marital counseling has revealed that it is one of the first symptoms to appear and last to come back (if and when the marriage improves significantly). So as the reader can readily see, the effects of avoidance tend to compound over time. What starts out as a negative response to perceived rejection, differences in values, conflict over parenting styles or division of labor in the home, etc., can mushroom into a huge division when there is a pattern of avoidance in dealing constructively with these issues. This is not to say that a singular issue will destroy the emotional fabric of a marriage. Rather, it is the cumulative effects of unattended and ineffectively addressed conflicts and disagreements that will create a chasm that will be difficult to bridge when too many years of avoidance take place. Recall that unpleasant events are more powerful than pleasant ones. Therefore, we can ruin 360 good days as a partner with 5 really bad ones!

A marriage is not unlike a home. If not maintained, it will eventually become dilapidated. Unfortunately, many couples wait too long to get help. By the time they get into counseling, it may be that painful experiences are not forgotten or forgiven, including a possible affair or more (yet another form of avoidance). At this point one or both partners may not have enough love remaining to be motivated to try to repair their relationship, even if they want to do so for the children's sake. They may simply decide it is easier and more sensible to knock the house down and start over, as opposed to having to rebuild the decimated structure left standing.

In order to avoid these types of negative consequences, it is vital that the couple maintain assertive communication of their feelings and thoughts while inhibiting the natural tendency to run and/or fight. This is not to say that it is never appropriate to walk away when too emotional to discuss feelings and thoughts constructively or that we should always avoid a "fair fight." However, even when very emotional, highly differentiated persons say what they mean and mean what they say. Communication is not meant to hurt or control. However, it is emotionally honest and delivered with a willingness to be understanding and open to negotiation and compromise. Obviously, we can't compromise on every issue (we can't have one and one-half kids!). So, sometimes one has to "win' (i.e., get their way). However, if we carry an attitude that marriage is a zero-sum game, then differences and conflicts are viewed as either I win or you win. Certainly, relationships will likely have less conflict and be more satisfying when partners maintain a win-win approach. In other words, we both win when we help our partner maximize their pleasure and try to find activities we find mutually satisfying. Certainly, it is easier to love someone who accepts us as we are, and can give and receive without taking things too personally or holding on to grudges (Church, Brooks & Kohlert, 2011).

Of course, a difficult situation arises when our partner continues to take advantage of us even though we regularly display non-avoiding and accepting styles of relating. What are we to do? This kind of dilemma is common and hits at the heart of our values and priorities of life. Much of what may be considered often depends on situational factors such as whether there are children, age, finances, etc. At any rate, it should be emphasized that long held patterns are not likely to change on their own. Accepting this reality is typically an important first step. Each member of the couple has the potential to see how their lack of differentiation enabled their mate to remain mired in a no-growth relationship and either can stop this dysfunctional process. Both have the responsibility to get help, individually and/or as a couple, get out of the relationship and/or stop the placations, non-assertive communications, hostility, withdrawal, etc., that has been established and maintained through habits and roles to which they are now accustomed. Once they stop avoiding the constructive paths available to them, they can see the truth. Does their mate really want an intimate, evolving relationship or do they want to stay stuck in mud? It may be that only then they can face and accept the answers they were afraid to confront while being too engaged in running and fighting patterns.

Dysfunctions of a Compulsive Nature

Admittedly, we are creatures of habit and prone to certain types of compulsive behavior patterns. Some are rather innocuous or inappropriate (e.g., nail biting) and others are generally constructive if not too excessive (e.g., organizing, exercising, working, cleaning). William Glasser refers to the constructive types as "positive addictions." However, some of us develop compulsive behavior patterns which, to varying degrees, represent avoidance/escape coping styles. As pointed out earlier in the book, these behaviors fall under the rubric of negative reinforcement. As a result, they become engrained aspects of our personality functioning (i.e., strong habits that have been learned and reinforced by the consequences of distraction and relief). They can often take the individual's attention and efforts away from important issues at hand and frequently mask and/or create depression due to their self-defeating nature. At best, they serve to distract us from upsetting emotions and stress but may lead to underachievement, poor relationships, self-destructive acts, legal problems, financial loss, and/or persistent negative emotional states. Common examples include excessive gambling, eating disorders, kleptomania, "internet addiction," self-mutilation and hoarding.

Individuals are frequently quite sensitive about these kinds of behavior. They tend to increase their compulsivity when highly stressed, particularly when alone. They tend to hide their compulsive patterns because they realize their inappropriateness but have difficulty in restraining these acts. Of course, others eventually find out about their compulsive acts thereby increasing their tendencies to avoid and escape (e.g., secretiveness, withdrawal) while giving them more reason to act compulsively. They are often caught in a vicious cycle they don't know how to change or stop. Moreover, a cascading effect of social, emotional, employment and/or legal issues may mount and become overwhelming, particularly when it all comes to light. They tend to have a good deal of shame and embarrassment about their compulsive patterns and how long they have been deceiving others about them. Don't forget, deception is yet another form of avoidance/escape!

Ultimately, their self-defeating coping can only be effectively addressed if they are motivated to significantly reduce their avoidance patterns.

Whether involved in self-help or therapeutically induced behavior changes, they need to face what they have been running from in order to facilitate the substitution of constructive thoughts and behaviors. Some frequent underlying issues revolve around low self-esteem, generalized anxiety/ insecurity, coping skill deficits, poor social skills, traumatic experiences and personality disorders.

Sexual Dysfunctions

There are several forms of sexual dysfunction, including disorders related to performance (impotence, vaginismus), paraphilias (inappropriate paths to sexual arousal such as exhibitionism and voyeurism), and hypoactive (less than expected) sexual desire. Lack of sexual desire is by far the most common sexual difficulty reported by both men and women, particularly the latter. What do these sexual disorders have in common; the old nemesis Avoidance of course! Avoidance patterns are almost assuredly either a primary or secondary causation to the establishment and maintenance of these kinds of sexual dysfunction. Moreover, many have a compulsive flavor to them along the lines of what we saw in the discussion above. This is especially true with the paraphilias (e.g., exhibitionists, voyeurs, fetishists). On the other hand, those with lack of desire show a penchant to avoid intimacy and/or sex. Whatever the case, the avoidance patterns that have developed cannot be effectively dealt with until there is acceptance of the core problems and openness to confronting whatever needs to be dealt with. Of course, each individual requires a somewhat different treatment approach designed to address their special needs. Those with hypoactive sexual desire provide a good example, as their underlying core issues tend to be many and varied, including but not limited to: boredom, poor communication, high levels of stress, medical problems, drug/alcohol/medication use, resentments, poor self-esteem, and low capacity for intimacy. Until these causative factors are managed more effectively, no amount of Viagra, sex toys, different partners, etc., will lead them out of their "maze to nowhere." By now, it is probably clear to the reader that one of the initial hurdles to overcome is the inertia caused by our natural resistance to change. Changes, even positive ones, are stressful and tend to be resisted. It seems easier to stick with the status quo and our habitual ways of doing things, unless we can find an easy remedy or pill to use. Although it takes a lot of motivation to overcome our defensiveness and the avoidance patterns that helped create self-defeating behaviors in the first place, it is the easier and more satisfying approach in the long haul. As we have discussed previously, a key element related to motivation is commitment to a self-chosen path. In this case motivation to give and receive in more complete and healthy ways can provide increased motivation to approach (pleasure), even if the face of strong avoidance (anxiety/fear) factors. Of course, the less engrained the avoidance patterns the better the prognosis. Other approach motives may include wanting to provide better role modeling and home atmosphere for the children. Mates who feel desired and connected with their partner tend to display more warmth and contentment. These qualities not only help stabilize a marriage but tend to make the home a more psychologically healthy and positive environment. Mates who share more intimacy are less likely to overcompensate with attention, affection and permissiveness toward one or more of their children which can throw the emotional and social climate in the home way out of kilter. They are also less likely to have affairs, watch pornography alone, and make negative comments about the other sex. At any rate, with sufficient motivation to change, the causes of longstanding psychosexual problems can be effectively addressed.

Chapter Seven

Paths to Increasing Acceptance

Thus far, we have been discussing acceptance primarily as a reactive process. That is, how can we use acceptance in ways that will help us adapt to unexpected stress, trauma, inappropriate developmental trends, negative situations, etc.? However, we need to realize that acceptance issues can be attacked proactively too because it is a "protective factor." That is, people who have developed a strong sense of how to accept problems of varying complexity and degree, including unexpected pitfalls, tend to be resilient when "shit hits the fan." They have the capacity to prevent the development of psychological disorders or, at the very least, mitigate the devastating effects of major life stressors. Moreover, they are much less likely to heap upon themselves problems that can grow like a cancer into a potentially lethal state.

We can envision the brain as somewhat analogous to a computer. Our genetics are prewired like the hard ware of a computer. The hardware is relatively immutable; it is what it is. However, software added and subtracted to the computer allows for modifications and enhancements and can be continuously updated and altered to address new problems or old ones in new ways, increase life satisfaction, alter perspectives, etc. Looked at in this way, we have the potential to change our software in ways that will better suit our wants and needs as we decide to make adjustments in how we think and act. These software elements can include self-dialogues that involve important issues of acceptance. They can be strengthened with repetition much like behavioral habits. Once strengthened, they become relatively permanent aspects of our personality that protect us, analogous to a vaccine for a disease. Certainly, no matter how we look at life and ourselves, there is realization that certain events and circumstances would "blow anyone out of the box." Nevertheless, when armed with realistic expectations and ways of looking at and reacting to life, we will almost assuredly fall less distance and experience a softer landing with expected or unexpected blows.

The points that follow are based upon almost 40 years of clinical work and more than 40 years of college teaching, not to mention personal experiences. They were chosen because, in this author's experience, they are some of the most common and crucial themes people struggle with that can cause and sustain chronic depression, as well as many other psychological disorders. Essentially, they cover key aspects of acceptance related to Self, Others, and Life. When these points of acceptance are rationally and emotionally accepted, we are much better prepared to live life according to the way it is, as opposed to being frustrated with why it isn't the way we think it should be.

This general topic reminds the author of when he first learned the importance of going with the flow rather than swimming against the tide. He and a friend tried to impress some teenage girls by swimming to a small island in a remote resort in Western Mexico. After being swept out about half way by a friendly tide, we found ourselves swimming against one. Rather than going with the tide, we foolishly chose to swim as hard as we could against it. All we managed to do was exhaust ourselves. Miraculously, a teenage boy paddling out in the middle of nowhere on a surfboard, managed to save our lives. He couldn't save our damaged egos though. Those on shore, including the girls we wanted to impress, couldn't help but become aware of what happened. Nevertheless there is something to be said about being humbled and making mistakes, especially ones we will never forget. A valuable lesson was learned that day about trying to be something we're not (i.e., a great swimmer), and how exhausting it can be when we try to go against the powerful tides of nature.

The acceptance-related propositions delineated below are categorized into three general areas, namely those most closely associated with Self, Others and Life. Although this breakdown is overlapping in some cases, it was felt that this type of classification would be more sensible and comprehensible than merely listing the 32 propositions independently, as if none of them shared common properties.

Basic Acceptance Issues

Acceptance Related to Self

1. **The most frequent path to chronic depression is avoidance.** Although there are many roads to chronic depression, this book highlights common ways people gradually back themselves into a depressive corner with their patterns of avoiding stress, responsibility, pain, anxiety/fears, etc. Seen in this way, chronic depression is generally not the problem per se but rather the side effect of maladaptive coping styles. Simply put, chronic depression is usually the result of patterns of avoidance and escape maneuvers, including key aspects of non-acceptance.

2. **The things we work hardest for are almost always those we have the greatest appreciation for.** It seems like a truism to say that nothing worthwhile in life is easy. Nevertheless, it is vital that we remind ourselves of this reality on a routine basis. It seems like almost every day we hear or read about someone who got caught doing something unethical or illegal because they lacked the patience and persistence required to meet long-term goals. By avoiding, bending and/or breaking rules or laws, they attempted to advance their power base, status and/or got involved in get rich schemes. Not only will these inappropriate and unethical methods rob us of contentment in the long run, they cause various types of legal and personal problems. We need to accept that the most important parts of life are labors of love (parenting, marriage, career, friendship, citizenship, spirituality).

3. **Positive behavior is more powerful than positive thinking with regard to maintaining and/or increasing self-esteem.** Although positive thinking can have important motivational influences on people with moderate to high self-esteem, the confidence, social feedback and productivity/creativity derived from constructive

behaviors is far more impactful than positive thought processes, particularly with people possessing low self-esteem. It may be pleasant to think about getting a hit but doing so has minimal effects on increasing self-esteem and confidence building. There is no substitute or better remedy for low self-esteem than effort and success. Effort is the only thing under our direct control and prerequisite to achievement and continued success.

4. **A life without purpose is a meaningless existence.** With few exceptions, people with chronic depression reveal a distinct lack of purpose for living and tend to and retreat from committed actions directed toward valued goals. Some of these individuals have even stopped engaging in hobbies or never really developed them. Many have withdrawn from social activities and are minimally involved in intimate relationships. Often, the best that these individuals can say when asked about their purposes is they live "day to day." They claim that they want to be "normal" and/or happy but act as if they can just hedonistically engage in the "present moment" and be content, without any concern that the future will soon drown them in their present. Most of us can relate to this in a relatively innocuous way by remembering how we occasionally blew off studying for an exam so we could have a good time with our friends or do something we wanted to more than study. Well, how did that work out when we found ourselves staring at an exam with a brain empty of knowledge? As discussed in the next chapter, there is a huge difference between happiness and contentment, the former being much more transient than the latter. We need to understand and accept the importance of working toward a life of contentment which can only be accomplished through long-term pursuit and persistence toward meeting self-defined goals.

5. **People learn to be pessimists, so they can learn to be optimists.** We've all observed children who believe that they can do things we know they cannot and have never even tried. It is not difficult for children to imagine themselves being a Hall of Famer in a sport or able to perform a skill they never practiced. At some

point, reality sets in and they realize it takes a combination of incredible genetic potential and hard work to reach the highest levels in any field. Along the way failure, rejection, disapproval and stiff competition can turn many children and adolescents into cynical pessimists regarding academics, marriage, friendship, and skill development. Nevertheless, as Seligman (1991) argued, we can return to a more balanced approach which he terms "learned optimism." From the vantage point of this book, this author prefers the phrase "realistic optimism." Certainly, there are many advantages to being optimistic but we need to caution ourselves to keep it within the realm of realistic expectations. Of course, what seems realistic can change over time in relation to many variables. So, changes in our awareness and insight can prompt us to change our perspectives of what is realistic in relation to self-observations and feedback from others we trust.

6. **Objects in the rearview mirror appear closer than they are (Steinman, 1994).** Memories of historical traumas are far from our present, even if it doesn't seem that way. We need to accept that just because we think and feel something from our past is being experienced in the present, that doesn't make it so. We are neither a helpless child, a naïve young adult, nor back in those situational contexts which traumatized us. By not letting go of the past, we rob ourselves of the present and have difficulty moving positively into our future. Interestingly, it is popular these days to encourage people to "live in the moment." While it is true that some people are so focused on the past or future they cannot enjoy and fully experience the present, it can also be argued that we need to learn from the past, appreciate our history and be guided by our goals and aspirations. Furthermore, aren't the past, present and future experienced in the present? So, rather than emphasize living in the moment, does it make more sense to stress the importance of balancing our experiences in these three realms while trying to ensure we are not manifesting Avoider qualities? Note here that a person could be an Avoider by focusing excessively on the "here and now."

7. **Regrets and hurts are lessons learned (Adele et. al., 2011).** Like it or not, we learn our most important lessons when we make mistakes and how not to repeat them. Mistakes in judgment and behavior can be quite humbling and hurtful, yet inevitable. We all make them. Still, the development of humility, in combination with the suffering and pain associated with it, allow us to grow as individuals and have more empathy when others make mistakes. These experiences are necessary parts of life and help us learn what not to do again, like not putting our hand in a fire. We need to accept that we usually learn more by doing things wrong than right!

8. **Acceptance is not giving up or quitting.** Acceptance is, however, acknowledgement of the reality of situations and the limits of what we can do about them. Often, we do not like our available alternatives but we always have at least two, and must live with the consequences of them. Generally, our alternatives include standing pat with the way we think or act, leaving or altering the situation if possible, or modifying the way we look at or react to the situation. We need to accept that changing the other person almost never works. Sometimes we are able to influence others but actual change in another's personality is something that only they can accomplish and is their responsibility. When confronted with unsavory situations, we frequently do not have control over the factors relevant to making effective change. Sometimes, we may leave or alter a situation as a way of adapting more positively and constructively to it. Frequently, our best option is accepting the situation or person which is also part and parcel of accepting that there is no solution or fix to the problem. In this case we haven't quit, we have simply accepted this as our best option.

9. **We cannot analyze or think too much.** We often hear people complain that they or others analyze things too much. However, closer analysis suggests that we cannot think too much. However, we can think in wrong ways. It is in our nature to analyze ourselves and others in order to try to figure out what is causing various

psychological and other phenomena. This is not something that we turn off easily, as it is in our nature. We've all experienced times when we don't want to think about certain problems or situations. We may even have trouble going to sleep because our brain is spontaneously generating alternative ways we can look at and react to certain situations, while calculating the ramifications of such. Even when we are asleep, our unconscious mind is working when we dream. In essence, our brain is rarely at rest. We need to accept that our brain is going to look for fixes and solutions whether or not we want it to or if they actually exist. Sometimes we can distract ourselves in order to minimize ruminations and analyses of situations. However, there are going to be times when we need to let our brain do its thing, especially with significant issues. This may lead to sleepless nights but that is to be expected sometimes. Once we acknowledge there is no fix or solution to the problem at hand and/or decide on how to handle a problem situation, we short circuit the ruminations and dwelling processes. Acceptance amounts to deciding on a course of action from our available alternatives which may include doing nothing if we decide the situation is not our problem/responsibility or unfixable. At any rate, when people say they or others are ruminating or analyzing too much, it is usually because they are not accepting something about their life. They are unproductively cycling through the same negative and/or unrealistic thought patterns, and/or not accepting that there is no remedy or solution to the problem or situation at hand.

10. **"The brave man is not he who does not feel afraid, but he who conquers that fear" (Mandela).** According to the late great Nelson Mandela, we should not evaluate ourselves based on whether we feel fear. Rather, we should evaluate ourselves with regard to what we do with that feeling. Essentially, this perspective reflects the notion that we all experience fear but not all of us cope with it effectively; that is, are capable of separating themselves from it. In other words, some display the capacity to experience fear without letting it define who they are (i.e., "I must

be a coward") or dominate their focus while, at the same time, continuing to move through their fear and toward the obtainment of valued goals. The more a person focuses on their fear, the more immobilized they will become. Although uncomfortable, fear it is not negative per se and can be viewed as not only natural but a positive aspect of our being. There are distinct advantages to fear, particularly survival oriented ones. Avoiding and escaping from fear on a regular basis can take us far afield from the valued paths we want to travel.

11. **Since we set rules up in our head, we can usually make ourselves winners.** It is a truism to state that we can't get something without giving something up. There is always some cost(s) associated with getting and/or keeping the things we want or have. As pointed out early in the book, life is full of ambivalent situations (e.g., approach vs. avoidance conflicts). We are often repelled and drawn by the same object, person or thing. Thus, it often seems that no matter what we choose to do, we lose. But this does not have to be the case. Suppose a friend asks you to help him move in a few weeks. You are torn because there are other things you were looking to do on that day but, at the same time, you would like to help your friend. You may set up the situation in your head so you lose no matter what you decide. In other words if you say yes, then you might be frustrated and, if you say no, you may feel guilty for not helping or living up to your feelings of obligation. An acceptance approach would set the framework up differently. From this perspective, you can set up the rules in your head so that you are at peace with either course of action. You can help your friend out with positive attitudes and perspectives, or let go of any negative feelings you may have for not living up to what is perceived as some kind of obligation. After all, you don't have to feel guilty about saying no to a request. You have a right to follow your self-interests, just as your friend does. A friend was requesting help not demanding it. Therefore, you have the right to say no if you so choose. This is merely a small example of how we have the

capacity to set the rules so that we win either way, as opposed to losing no matter what choice is made.

12. **We are stronger than we think during times of extreme stress.** We need to accept that our bodies and minds are built to withstand great amounts of stress, particularly over relatively short periods of times. Sometimes we need to trust in ourselves that we will be okay. Often, we hear people say things like: "I can't take anymore," "I am on my last nerve," or "Reserve a bed in the nearest psych ward." At times like these, we need to remind ourselves of how we have coped in the past. These examples of negative thinking above are reactions to feeling overwhelmed and need to be seen as just that; not facts. More than likely, our history will remind us of how we've always adapted and survived. It is important to reinforce our thoughts of self-efficacy (i.e., I am a competent and adaptable person, capable of handling almost anything that comes my way). Giving in to feeling overwhelmed by being dependent or quitting will lead to poor coping skills and self-fulfilling prophecies. Certainly, caving in will not lead to greater confidence and is likely to increase our avoidance of stress in the long run.

Acceptance Related to Others

13. **Few things in life are personal.** Although we may believe that people often try to put us down, frustrate and manipulate us, the reality is that most people are simply acting in their self-interest. What we envision as personal attacks are more likely due to competition, differences in personality, miscommunication, and/ or self-preoccupation. If someone cuts us off with their car, our natural reaction is probably fear or anger, along with a tendency to take what happened personally. We might even react with some form of aggression or road rage. However, except in very special circumstances, the other driver doesn't even know us. How could it be personal? Most likely, the other driver was preoccupied, didn't

see us or was experiencing time pressures or an emergency. At any rate, we just happen to be in the wrong place at the wrong time.

14. **We're not in this world to live up to others' expectations of us and they are not in it to live up to ours' (Perls, 1976).** On the contrary, we each have the unique responsibility to be authentic with ourselves by being who we truly are. One of the quickest ways to be dissatisfied in life is to try to be someone we're not. Resisting pressure to be what others want us to be can be difficult, but failure to do so will almost assuredly lead to depression, underachievement and inauthenticity.

15. **In giver-taker relationships there isn't a "good guy."** Both givers and takers extract things from the other that are inappropriate, unfair and/or they could get on their own. Eventually, both blame the other for their own internal prohibitions. Neither givers nor takers exhibit a balanced personality (i.e., give and take) which is necessary for relationships to grow (Church, Brooks and Kohlert, 2011). Thus, each tends to hold the other back while not allowing themselves or significant others the opportunity to learn how to develop and maintain effective and intimate long-term relationships. At the same time, they almost certainly make their job as caretakers more difficult as kids learn how to divide, conquer and perpetuate conflicts rather than resolve them. What is the acceptance challenge here? Typically, it begins with the realization that "benign neglect" of marital schisms is not a solution. Things are not likely to get better on their own. If problems do not spontaneously resolve, then there are only a few alternatives available. We can leave things as they are, attempt to change them (e.g., engage in self-help or counseling) or alter the situation (e.g., separate or divorce). If our partner is not willing to work with us to try to establish a more balanced relationship, then we need to either peacefully accept this type of mutual co-existence or do something about it. Continuing to internally grind over differences and fight over things we cannot change or control simply is a self-defeating strategy.

16. **It is unreasonable to expect people to act inconsistently.** On the surface, this may appear to be an odd statement. However, clinical experience has taught the author that many people react with surprise when others frustrate, reject or even abuse them or others on a regular basis. They will say things like; "I can't believe he/she acted this way again," or "I can't understand how someone could do such a thing." Of course, the therapist is the one who should be surprised at this point by such statements, and will likely challenge the client by pointing out they are not accepting the reality of their history with certain people and how personalities operate. Research is clear in demonstrating that people tend to be cognitively and behaviorally consistent, particularly across similar situations (Aronson, 2013). Thus, the best prediction of a person's future behavior is their past behavior. Unless we have substantial evidence that a person has changed, then we should expect them to behave in ways consistent with their past, and be surprised when they don't!

17. **Most psychological problems are relationship-oriented (Glasser, 1998).** This author's clinical experience has been consistent with William Glasser's assertion that relationship dysfunctions underlie most psychological problems. Most people treated in inpatient psychiatric facilities and with outpatient psychological services have significant problems in initiating, establishing and/ or maintaining effective and intimate relationships at home and/or work. With regard to marital functioning, Glasser maintains that couples are bound to have core differences in personality needs. No couple is perfectly matched. Since core personality needs are likely to change little over time, these differences will need to be resolved through empathetic and assertive communication, compromise, negotiation and acceptance. Unfortunately, if both partners are not willing to accept that these postures are necessary for the smooth long-term functioning of the couple, then this type of avoidance will tend to lead to the destruction of the relationship by way of endless conflicts and resentments, lowered fun and intimacy, and a loss of perceived freedom.

18. **People pleasers do not really please others much.** First and foremost, people pleasers are people too and they do a poor job at pleasing themselves. They frequently feel taken advantage of and disrespected. This is due to their penchant to bend over backwards with others while generating little with respect to their ideas and creativity, as well as avoiding conflict and controversy. As a result, others rarely consider the merits of their opinions or feelings. Ultimately, they complain about being taken for granted but fail to appreciate how they "rip off" others by not allowing them to bond effectively with a "whole person" with whom they can grow mutually.

Acceptance Related to Life

19. **Feelings are merely feelings and thoughts are just thoughts.** Many of our thoughts and feelings occur spontaneously, and vary extensively with situational context and moods. As vital as they are to our being human, we need to keep in mind that they are not facts. They are not valid representations of reality. All of us have unusual and disturbing thoughts now and then. We should not make too much of these thoughts and feelings unless they are disturbing and become stronger and more frequent, or lead to an intention and plan to do harm to self and/or others. We have thousands of thoughts daily. If just .001 percent of our thoughts are hostile, strange or disturbing, so what? This is to be expected. The author has had numerous people come into therapy because of a single disturbing thought which was clearly out of character for them. The more they tried to suppress it, the more frequently it occurred and the more distressed they became over it. Once they accepted the crucial distinction between thoughts vs. actions, and acknowledged such thinking was both common and natural, they were able to calm down and accept their disturbing thoughts as essentially innocuous and spontaneous (i.e., part of being human). In turn, the distressing thoughts diminished significantly. Of course, if disturbing thoughts are experienced on a continuous

basis and cannot be "let go," then there is good reason to believe that appropriate professional help is in order.

20. **Life isn't a popularity contest.** We don't need hundreds or thousands of "friends" on Facebook. We couldn't be real friends with that many people anyway. Getting attention and adoration from multitudes of others may boost our ego temporarily, but is superficial at best. We only need a few intimate friends and family members. The more thinly we spread ourselves with superficial interactions, the less energy and time we have to devote to our meaningful relationships. Millions of adoring fans were not enough to keep Marilyn Monroe, Michael Jackson and numerous other famous people alive. Clearly, many people avoid crucial aspects of life that, when not dealt with effectively, lower the quality and quantity of living.

21. **Love is not enough.** We are regularly fed the notion that "love conquers all" via movies, songs and other forms of media. Yet, the reality is that there are many we could fall in love with that we cannot live with amicably and love long-term. Simply put, some relationships do not possess the right chemistry or commitment. Ham and cheese and ham and eggs go well together but what about ham and apricots? Is there anything wrong with apricots, or do they just not go with ham? Along a somewhat different vein, will our love help someone get over an addiction who is not motivated sufficiently? Certainly, love can be a powerful force in determining individual behavior and relationship interactions. Nevertheless, the reality is that there are limits to what love or any other emotion can conquer.

22. **Most psychological problems, like medical ones, are not fixable.** Rather, most psychological problems are emotionally based and primarily amenable to acceptance-based approaches. Therefore, rather than seeing a therapist as someone who will solve or help fix our problems, it is usually more accurate to envision the therapist as helping us to better accept our suffering, manage our

problems, avoid future mistakes, and make better choices. If our problems were essentially logically based, then people wouldn't need help with self-destructive and self-defeating behavior patterns, like suicide, smoking cigarettes, compulsive gambling and unsafe sex. A computer, hardwired with a program of self-preservation, would never engage in these types of behaviors. Human beings, on the other hand, frequently engage in self-defeating behavior patterns based primarily on impulsivity, short-sided hedonism and/or negative emotional states, such as anxiety, envy, jealousy, anger, etc., all of which are generally inconsistent with rational thinking. Clinical experience shows that most interpersonal conflict, including marital disagreements, occurs over issues of preference (e.g., attitudes, interests, beliefs, values) where there is no actual right versus wrong. Interestingly, most couples in marital counseling have difficulty recounting the last time they had an argument over something important. If their problems were factually based, they could look up the "right" answers in a book. Once again, this point highlights the vital roles of acceptance with respect to our individual and relationship problems.

23. **Life isn't fair; it is what it is.** Although it is easy to rationally agree with this statement, how many of us actually accept it emotionally? Just because we accept something rationally doesn't mean we fully accept it because, in order for this to occur, it has to be accepted on an emotional basis. For example, humans come to accept that they will die. However, this does not mean that a person faced with a terminal illness will be able to emotionally accept his or her fate without a considerable amount of emotional work. Kubler-Ross (1969) and others outlined the stages of dying that people tend to go through with acceptance being the last stage. It can take a substantial amount of time for us to reach a point of full acceptance. Some never do. They run out of time or don't have the capacity to do so. One of this author's clients, diagnosed with cancer, spoke about his "condition" while never using the term cancer. He died about a year after being diagnosed

with pancreatic cancer and never got out of the first stage of the dying process, denial.

24. **The most powerful learning principle effect on the development of psychological disorders is negative reinforcement.** As pointed out earlier, negative reinforcement includes both avoidance and escape from unpleasant experiences. Since unpleasant experiences tend to be much more powerful than pleasant ones in reinforcing behavior, they can dominate the pursuit of pleasant experiences, especially as we get closer to a goal object. Since most goals are associated with both pleasant and unpleasant stimuli, approach versus avoidance conflicts are routine aspects of living. People frequently tell us how badly they want to change but, irrespective of their perceived rewards for doing so, have been unable to overcome their patterns of avoidance. Thus, it will be vital for them to either work on reducing impact of avoidance forces and/or increasing their willingness to confront and move through the ambivalence of avoidance vs. approach.

25. **People are neither rational nor irrational; rather, they are rationalizing.** As Aronson (2013) has emphasizes, humans have the capacity to utilize a variety of cognitive methods which allow them to see the world in ways they want or need to see it, as opposed to how it really is. Via the use of various cognitive distortions and defensive postures, like denial and rationalization, people have the capacity to justify almost any attitude, belief or action. Underlying motivation for attitudes and behaviors are primarily driven by our need to protect our self-esteem, perceive we are "right," and have a sense of mastery/control over ourselves and our environments (Aronson, 2013). Although we rationally know that there are no two people in the world that possess the same sets of attitudes, beliefs and values, it is difficult for us to accept that our ways of viewing the world are not the "right ones."

26. **Suffering is painful but can give meaning to life and promotes survival.** Of course, it is natural to try to avoid or escape from

painful experiences. However, as Victor Frankl pointed out in his classic work <u>Man's Search for Meaning</u> (1962), even situations of long-term suffering can have benefits. Such situations can bring out the best in us, teach us more about life, and bring us closer to those suffering similar fates. Moreover, the energy provided by our suffering can be transformed into positive and constructive motivations and behaviors. Recall that we discussed the positive benefits of anger in an earlier section. It is not uncommon for us to see people turn their lives around after hitting rock bottom. Realistically speaking, self-initiated change is difficult and tends to be preceded by a large dose of self-disgust. So, it is unlikely that a person will stop using cigarettes, begin exercising routinely, make significant changes in their study habits, etc. until they suffer a certain degree of self-contempt. It is difficult to make changes when things are mediocre or average. Put another way, mostly anyone can look for a job when they don't have one or are miserable with their current employment. On the other hand, it could be very difficult to seek employment when we perceive our job is okay. The same is often true with marriage, friendship, residence, etc.

27. **Life rarely turns out the way we expect it to, and that is usually positive.** While an undergraduate student, one of the author's psychology professors made a statement along this vein on the first day of class. It seemed rather incredulous at the time. However, this professor knew we weren't expecting him to be the teacher. We signed up thinking it would be taught by a renowned psychologist who wrote the textbook required for the class. Most of us knew that the textbook was considered the "gold standard" for this course. He heard our sighs when he walked into class and decided to give us another way to look at the situation. He reminded us that the other professor might have little to tell us beyond what he already articulated in the required book and he planned to give us some "other points of view." As it turned out, it was the most interesting class this author took as an undergraduate! So, it didn't take long to experience an example of his wisdom.

28. **Nothing psychological is 100%.** No one can give 100% daily to anything. We are not machines and even they break down. Loyalty, trust, love, friendship, honesty, etc. are not discrete 0% or 100% facets. We sometimes hear people say that they gave 110% to something. When we actually think objectively about this type of statement, we realize how absurd it is. The best we can expect from ourselves and others is essential trust, honesty, love, etc. which falls somewhere in the 95 to 99% range. We all make mistakes, are fallible, experience low moods and get ill. No one can guarantee that they will work at a 100% level every day, never tell a lie or always act lovingly. To expect such things is tantamount to setting ourselves and others up for disappointment and frustration. Furthermore, people who tend to perceive psychological processes in 100% fashion will tend to go to 0% when their expectations are violated. For example, a person who is lied to and or cheated on will tend to go from a naïve 100% to an extreme 0%, alleging they can no longer trust their partner or believe anything they say. Clearly, both 100% and 0% perspectives are erroneous.

29. **We are not ping pong balls.** We don't get slapped around by destiny, bad luck or fate. Yes, sometimes it seems like we can't even buy a break and the whole world is against us. Unlike ping pong balls, we are largely masters of our own fate. Unlike ping pong balls, we are all unique confluences of our heredity and environment and are challenged to make a multitude of choices, from the most innocuous to monumental. Unlike ping pong balls, we live with the consequences of our decisions and, hopefully, learn from and don't repeat them. Unlike ping pong balls, we not only make choices but are guided by a sense of meaning and purpose reflected in our goal directed behaviors. Unlike ping pong balls, we have a legacy which will be determined by our decisions and behaviors. Our legacy, of course, is reflected by how others have been impacted by our life and how we are remembered. Whether we choose to create and perpetuate constructive or destructive influences within our families, work environments, friendships and community, these ripple effects will continue to be passed on

long after we're gone. We are all part of a grand and continuous thread of life wherein we move from receiving from others as a relatively helpless infant and child to an adult who possesses the capacity to not only receive but to give back. Unlike ping pong balls, whether we want to accept this reality or not, it is our ultimate choice. Moreover, we always have more than one choice and typically at least three. When we feel trapped and without a choice, we to need to remember there are always alternative perspectives and actions, namely: we can do nothing different and continue to "grind" over it, accept our situation and work with it as best as possible, or try to change or influence the situation or person(s) involved which may or may not be realistic and could involve leaving the situation/person(s).

30. **We rarely know precisely why anyone does anything, including ourselves.** Although we can generally say that our behavior is due to the inevitable interaction between our genetics and environment, we never know precisely how they combine. Clearly, there are certain behaviors that are almost entirely determined by genetics, like walking upright and various reflexes. On the other hand, environment plays powerful roles the development of personality styles, including aspects of social and emotional development. However, when we try to get specific with causes of these aspects of behavior, analysis breaks down quickly due to the complexity of variables involved. As B. F. Skinner (1974) pointed out, we cannot know our precise genetics (or someone else's) nor can we know all of the environmental experiences in our history that impinge on a given behavior at a given point in time. Even if we knew the multitude of genetic and environmental variables that determine even simple choices and behaviors, we could not calculate the interactive effects of heredity and environment anyway. The human brain is not set up to specifically know these things. So, if someone likes chocolate ice cream, they could never know precisely why It seems like a pretty simple question, but is it? Let's say they respond with: "I must have been born with an aversion to it." Well, how do you know that? Is it possible that

you got sick after eating too much of it when you were four years old, and don't even remember this taste aversion experience? Or, is it possible that you have always liked to be different than the crowd and, when presented with vanilla, strawberry or chocolate at birthday parties, you chose strawberry because most of the other kids chose chocolate? Or, is it possible that two or three of these non-mutually exclusive alternatives combine with varying degrees of influence on you preferences? The fact is that we will never know precisely why we engage in even simple behavioral repertoires. Now, try to imagine how explaining the precise reasons for more complex decisions and behaviors. Therefore, it appears that the best we can do is guess why we and others do what they do. That's okay as long as we accept the reality of our hypotheses (i.e., they are not facts) and do not spend too much unproductive time or energy focused on "why". The "why" may be incorrect and doesn't change the nature of our alternative reactions to situation any way. This is especially tricky when we ask ourselves why someone else did what they did or assume we "know," because we are all unique and do things for different reasons. To the extent that we tend to project our ways of looking at and reacting to the world on to others, we can be way off target when we assume that others perceive and respond to things like we do. For example, we may play fair with others and expect the same, not realizing the rules of the game are "anything goes" in their ballpark. Therefore, rather than emphasize "why" questioning we recommend asking "what" is going on and "what," if anything, can be done to change or ameliorate the situation. As you might expect, this approach is more likely to lead to acceptance than asking why, especially when we decide there is little or nothing we can done to improve a given situation.

31. **Death is the primal fear of humans (Becker, 1973) but our most mundane and pervasive fears are related to people, particularly as they relate to abandonment and rejection.** Death is like a black cloud that hangs over us like a huge storm that will someday envelope each of us. This is an inescapable fate and, although

extremely difficult for most to accept, we need to figure out not only what life means but the meaning of death too. According to Becker, humans tend to deny the reality of death with a plethora of defensive postures in a futile effort to minimize anxiety and our inevitable confrontation with this unbeatable foe. As ominous as death can be, there is a fear that seems more pervasive in our daily lives, fear of being abandoned or hurt by others. More specifically, clinical experience has taught this author that what we fear most are rejection, embarrassment, disapproval, shame, jealousy, abandonment and other negative reactions related to others. Note that the latter (abandonment) overlaps Becker's analysis, as death is the pinnacle form of abandonment; separation and everything we know. Recently, a client of the author was almost was killed when his tractor rolled over his body. Miraculously, he survived without life threatening injures. A few months later he questioned how the breakup with a girlfriend of several months created more suffering that the psychological and physical pain caused by the tractor. This is but one example of how powerful the influence of separation and abandonment are on the human psyche. Toward the end of life, we find many people fear becoming a "vegetable" more than death. Among other reasons they give is that they do not want to be a burden on others. They know they have to die but they hope that they don't have to suffer the insults associated with not being able to care for themselves. Once again, we see the impact of fears associated with having to undergo possible feeling of dependency, humiliation abandonment, loneliness, etc. Very few people come into therapy to address fear of heights, insects, flying, elevators, job loss, etc. The vast majority of people who come into therapy with some form of fear are facing loneliness, separation (e.g., mourning, divorce, moving), psychological and/or physical abuse, rejection, guilt, jealousy, envy, shame, etc. Research support for this type of analysis comes from the correlation of life change units and significant medical problems. Holmes and Rahe (1967) rank ordered the most stressful life events and showed that there is a strong correlation between how much change we have undergone, and significant health-related problems that occur the following year. In other words, people who experienced the highest amounts of stress related to life changes were most likely to suffer significant illnesses during the subsequent year. Interestingly, most of the top ten stressors involved separation/abandonment issues (e.g., retirement, jail term, separation, divorce, death of a significant other). Anecdotal support for this type of analysis comes from the all-too familiar reactions of people who suffer from significant amounts of teasing, bullying, rejection and social isolation. We routinely hear about children, adolescents or young adults who explode with rage after being subjected to negativity from others for some time. More often than not, evidence suggests that these suicide and/or homicide attempts are not impulsive but rather deliberate and planned "executions." At least for some period of time, these sufferers were less afraid of dying than continuing to live in their present state of discontent with fear of abuse, loneliness and alienation. These observations are further testimony to the enormous power of avoidance and escape forces. Perhaps, if these sufferers had reached out for help earlier and/or those close to them recognized their pain and need for support, then tragedies could have been averted. Of course, perpetrators of teasing, bullying, intimidation and other forms of rejection and psychological torment also bear responsibility for their forms of avoidance. They either kept themselves unaware of the dynamics which drove their displacement of prejudice and hostility on to others, and/or failed to accept and address their own underlying psychological problems (e.g., need to elevate themselves at the expense of others).

32. **Winning isn't as important as most people think.** We often hear that "winning is everything" but may not think about what this truly means. In a bottom line society, wherein we exalt "winners," it may be difficult to look at this issue objectively and with the complexity is deserves. For example, how important is it to "win" a job or get a date that isn't a good fit? Do we really win when we don't play fair? Doesn't everyone who tries hard and plays by the rules win? After all, there can only be one winner and

the only factor we can control directly is our effort. From these perspectives, isn't winning just frosting on the cake? Furthermore, isn't a "loser" who displays sportsmanship and principles more of a winner than someone who lies, uses banned substances to enhance performance, cheats, steals or in some other way circumvents ethics or the rules? Thus, it is vital to remind ourselves that, win or lose, we should be proud of ourselves when we do our best and play fair.

Chapter Eight

Recommendations for Significant Others

Thus far, we have focused mainly on how the individual and therapist can effectuate appropriate and desired therapeutic changes. However, there has also been some mention of parental, marital and friendship involvements and how they relate to the reinforcement or mitigation of avoidance patterns and non-acceptance postures.

This chapter briefly outlines and explicates some of the most instrumental aspects of positive influence on the part of the significant others. Prior to outlining and discussing these important points, a few key ones should be mentioned. First, it should be noted that these orientations, strategies and/or interventions may be utilized with or without involvement in formal marital, family or support group counseling. Secondly, as will become apparent, many of these guidelines are more educational than therapeutic per se. Along this vein, since most of us have learned that an ounce of prevention is worth a pound of cure, an early foundation of helping children and adolescents develop constructive and realistic perspectives with regard to avoidance and acceptance issues becomes crucial to their long-term physical and psychological development. Finally, there is probably nothing more important than modeling appropriate and mature behavior, irrespective of role. So, whether we are a parent, spouse, friend, teacher, nurse, volunteer, etc., we need to do more than talk the talk.

Psychology has demonstrated overwhelmingly the power of modeling effects on the development and maintenance of attitudes, values, beliefs and behavior. Therefore, if we want to be a good parent, we need to be a good person, first and foremost. The same could be said of our other roles. Can we expect to have good friends if we're not one? For the most part, we get what we deserve. Furthermore, it is easy to tell people to not avoid stress, pain, responsibility, etc. but it is another thing to actually face difficult life changes, decisions, conflicts and fears. Naturally, we want to avoid or put off such things and struggle with cognitive, emotional and behavioral acceptance for a multitude of reasons, including the anxiety that accompanies life's uncertainties and the length of time required to fully accept certain realities. An example of this process is seen often with couples who are in gridlock. As Schnarch points out in his classic work *Passionate Marriage* (1997), we don't get ready for marriage, marriage gets us ready for marriage! In other words, we can only grow as individuals and as a couple together; communicating, adjusting, compromising, negotiating and accepting our differences and conflicts. He envisions a couple like two mountain climbers who can only climb as fast and high as the slowest because they are linked by a common line. Of course, the temptation we all have to deal with at times is the desire to run and/or fight when we feel afraid or overwhelmed. Unfortunately, the over-utilization of these reactions does not facilitate positive development for the individual or couple. Rather, it makes their situation worse in many ways and does not lead to better avenues. In this kind of situation the slowest climber needs to pick up the pace, face their tendencies to avoid and/or blame, and the faster climber needs to resist letting the slower one drag them down or take advantage of the lower functioning one. Otherwise, they are at best at an impasse and no-growth option. They will soon have very few safe topics to talk about and will be most likely living with very little intimacy. Note that his type of psychological gridlock can occur in all types of relationships.

Having set the stage for articulation of appropriate perspectives and strategies with respect to inappropriate acceptance and avoidance patterns, numerous general recommendations are advanced (see below): Note that the emphasis to be applied will vary greatly depending on the situational context, age(s), maturity level, personality styles, therapeutic considerations, etc. of the individuals involved.

1. **Be assertive.** – This especially important in family life and in raising children. Kids are not likely to learn to be assertive in

school. So, if they don't learn how at home, where will they? Assertiveness is emotionally honest (and non-avoidant). And, most of us have learned that not only is honesty usually the best policy, the truth usually comes out in the end anyway.

2. **Walk the walks of non-avoidance and acceptance.** – We can't expect those close to us to do things we don't. We need to model non-avoidance and acceptance patterns for both ourselves and others. The effects of modeling are quite powerful, largely because they are subtle and produce little resistance. Modeling is rarely viewed by the observer as controlling, manipulative, bribing, threatening or intimidating, so it produces minimal rebellion or opposition. The observer is free to emulate the model or not. Research shows that we tend to model after people we look up to in some important ways.

3. **Don't enable avoiders.** – We don't help others when we enable their non-acceptance of reality. Avoiders tend to be good at justifying their self-defeating patterns by playing the victim, acting impish and/or blaming others. We need to not reinforce these inappropriate behaviors and perspectives while helping Avoiders see and cope with the underlying core issues driving avoidance and non- acceptance. We saw this repeatedly in the Case Studies presented where individuals hid behind their "addictions," psychiatric diagnoses, medicinal "solutions," dependency and other avoidant patterns.

4. **Don't be afraid to use leverage.** – Leverage is a powerful and widespread influence in life and not confined to the business world (Egan, 2010). Whether we are dealing with relatively innocuous behaviors such as lack of punctuality or procrastination or more serious ones like "addictions," the bottom line is "talk is cheap." Don't forget that consequences speak loudest. Whether it is a letter of reprimand that goes into an employee's file or we choose to leave the habitually late behind, sometimes avoiders need something else to avoid (i.e., appropriate consequences) in order to develop

sufficient motivation to change. Realistically, this is often the case in marital counseling too. Until and unless the non-avoidant partner leaves or shows a definite willingness to leave or stand their ground on issues, nothing more significant than temporary appeasements may change. Although clients often look at therapists as change agents, the reality is that psychotherapists do not possess leverage beyond emotionally-based sources of connection such as; accountability, approval, support and appreciation for knowledge. On the other hand, each partner has considerable leverage over the other whether they perceive it that way or not. Similar things could be said of parents who feel they don't have any leverage with their kids. The question is: Are they willing to use it or are they avoiding using leverage for some reason(s)?

5. **Emphasize effort rather than outcome.** – Repeatedly, we have covered examples of how crucial it is to emphasize that we can directly control effort, as opposed to outcomes. Thinking and communication needs to revolve around whether substantial effort was manifest, as opposed to; "Did I/you get the "A," date, job or touchdown. Focusing on effort not only helps preserve self-esteem during down periods but also facilitates positive motivation toward goal directed behavior.

6. **Focus on both short and long-term goals.** – As we know, our life situation contexts, roles, environments, demands, biology and personality needs shift throughout life. If we don't make proper adjustments to these realities, we almost certainly will become unhappy and discontent while drifting through life like an Avoider. We need to have short and long-term goals that give us a reason to pop out of bed in the morning with a sense of purpose, as opposed to being the type of person who acts like they just exist and then wonders why they don't feel alive. The latter is likely to ruminate excessively or unproductively about the past or simply look for distracting pleasure in the moment (e.g., over-eating, shop alcoholism, gambling, drug/alcohol abuse, etc.). Oppositely, the former is likely to cope with stress much better because they

have a sense of purpose for dealing with the challenges of life. Additionally, they are much more likely to achieve their goals and feel better about themselves, making them a more animated and positive person to be around. Thus, positive momentum (as opposed to the negative type seen with Avoiders) will tend to build and be sustained by predominantly non-avoidant and accepting behaviors and perspectives. Note that purposes don't have to be magnanimous. Small things count too. Hobbies and small leisure activities give us things to look forward to daily. The author has been surprised by how many people he has worked with who either do not have hobbies or fail to engage in them. Likewise, he has been struck by how many people do not regularly make the time to do something relaxing alone or with others on a regular basis. The cumulative effect of engaging in these types of positive activities can be as important as working toward highly valued long-term issues.

Chapter Nine

Reflections

Psychology has obviously come a long way since the beginning of the 20th Century. From the roots of Freudian analysis and Pavlov's classical conditioning, psychological theory and research has developed and expanded like a fledgling tree that has become massive. Along the way, psychologists have tested many assumptions, some commonsensical, in order to separate myth from reality. At the same time, many theories have been born but perished in attempts to explain the complexities of psychological functioning. During the middle portion of the 20th century, theorists and researchers tended to break away from Freud's psychodynamic theory and other unitary models were constructed and tested. Amongst those that survived, humanistic theories focused on the self-concept and actualization of personality. Behaviorists concentrated on how learning principles shape our personalities. Meanwhile, existentialists zeroed in on the how humans need to confront the inevitable anxiety that comes with uncertainty, particularly as it relates to abandonment and aloneness. In their own way, each of these approaches was narrow and exclusive in orientation. Further, some have been viewed as overly simplistic because they envision human behavior as explainable with simple constructs, especially behaviorism. Behaviorists looked at us as organisms responding relatively automatically to stimuli based upon previous experiences that were reinforcing or punishing. Eventually, this approach was expanded to include cognitions because it became clear that any comprehensive model of human behavior must include thinking. Surely, we are more than just a passive organism responding to stimulation, reinforcement or punishment!

Our thoughts not only mediate behavior via goals and self-control strategies but also play an important role in how we evaluate ourselves. Eventually, these developments led us to see the vital role of modeling on human behavior and, more broadly, the development of cognitive behavioral psychology. During the past twenty years or so, a "third wave" of cognitive behavioral psychology has developed and received significant support from researchers and clinicians. The approach, unlike the ones discussed above, represents a blending of several major ones that preceded it. In particular, ACT includes significant elements of existentialism, traditional cognitive behaviorism and humanism. Although there is still have a long way to go, some realities have remained relatively constant. One of those is that we are hedonistic beings. We are built to avoid pain and approach pleasure. Whether we use Freudian terms like oral gratification or superego to represent pleasure and pain, respectively, or behaviorism's reinforcement and punishment, the bottom line is the same. We are designed to maximize our pleasure and minimize pain. Nevertheless, we are very complicated and unique in creation, making our behavior very difficult to predict. Some of us will risk great amounts of pain in order to help ourselves or others obtain a goal with a high degree of personal value. Others do very little to maximize their pleasure or get little or no satisfaction from primary drives such as food and sex, irrespective of the strength of avoidance forces. On the surface, this may lead some to throw up their hands and say that human behavior is simply too complex to understand. After all, isn't everything determined by individual choice? Of course, just because we make choices doesn't mean our decisions are not subject to causation. As a science, psychology assumes our thoughts and behaviors are determined by the interaction between genetic and environmental variables. Since no two people have the same interaction between these two multi-factorial influences, human behavior across situations is extremely difficult to explain and predict. Thus, unitary approaches are obviously limited in their predictive and explanatory capacities.

Another constant and unshakable theme is that humans, unlike so-called lower animals, can visualize the future. We are aware of our mortality, biological clock, uncertainties of life, etc. We know illnesses, accidents, separations, and other unexpected events can derail us at any time. So, unlike a dog or cat, our prominent emotion is anxiety as opposed to fear. Uncertainties are inescapable and often painful but, at the same time, can be positive influences. Some of our best performances come when the chips are down and we're extremely anxious. Furthermore, if there wasn't uncertainty and we knew what was going to happen tomorrow, then would there be a purpose for living? Would we experience excitement and surprise? Or, would we simply be living out a role like an actor on the stage? Moreover, humans can envision a future, and possess the capability of developing a set of goals anchored in values that give their lives a sense of purpose. This is not simply following a path toward maximizing physiological pleasure. Rather, it amounts to developing plans and goals, creatively designed, that make living worthwhile. These goals help us face difficult tasks and responsibilities and even endure pain and distress on regular bases. Often, values and goals will be adjusted in response to changing circumstances because, without a clear sense of them, we are essentially drifting. By example, what good does it do to have a sail worthy boat if it travels aimlessly in the ocean? And, imagine a sail boat traveling around the world that is just a few degrees off course. How far off would it be in reaching its destination by the time it traveled around the world? The same could be said about our lives and how important it is to chart courses and adjustments along the way. This brings us back to a distinction made earlier between happiness and contentment. People who approach pleasure and/or avoid discomfort may be temporarily happier than they would be if they faced stressors that take them down valued long-term paths. However, contentment is satisfying too and more stable than happiness which is typically fleeting. This doesn't mean that a life concerned with maximizing present happy feelings is inherently wrong or bad, and one oriented toward long-term goals and purposes is judged to be right or good. Also, there is no implication here that a person cannot or shouldn't balance his/her life with present vs. future goals and pleasure. Rather, these points are made to emphasize that at least some areas of psychology are being inclusive in their analyses of short vs. long-term motivation and satisfaction, like ACT, and this type of approach is paying dividends for many people. Happiness is temporary and can be lost or taken from us at any time. Contentment, on the other hand, can only be gained through persistence toward long-term goals and is a relatively permanent part of our subjective experiences and history.

Having made the statements above, it seems ironic to say that looking back may be at least as important as looking forward. As existentialists point out, because the future is uncertain, we all have to cope with what they refer to as existential anxiety. That is, the foreboding that something terrible could happen to us or one of our loved ones at any time. Clinical experience demonstrates that people can find it very beneficial to sometimes look at both sides of the coin at the same time. In other words, we often experience less anxiety and more constructive motivation when looking simultaneously at our lives retrospectively and prospectively. For example, when we ask ourselves to imagine how we want our epitaph or eulogy to read, our focus is directed toward obtaining (approaching) goals with an eye on imagining ourselves in the past, as opposed to looking at our present anxieties and fears. The mountain looks very different looking downward (retrospectively). Avoidance forces are always present but don't seem so insurmountable when viewed from the top of the mountain.

We have long known that prospective thought plays instrumental roles in our effective functioning and degrees of life satisfaction. Although ACT emphasizes the importance of being mindful in the present moment, it is becoming increasingly clear that our imagination plays a fundamental role in our personality development and capacity to function effectively. Early theorists like Freud and Jung spent a great deal of time on dream analysis which they believed was a road to understanding the unconscious mind. Today, psychologists are investigating the role of daydreaming which a more of a conscious state. Daydreaming was once thought to be simply an unproductive form of distraction. Now, we see the crucial role it can play in facilitating positive or negative motivations and behaviors. Three types of daydreamers have been identified (Kaufman, 2004). One type exhibits "poor attention control" and is easily distracted with poor concentration. These individuals have a difficult time concentrating on both the external environment and their own internal thoughts. Generally, they are low in conscientiousness. A second type of daydreamer is called guilt-dysphoric. This type tends to be neurotic and full of anxiety, guilt, hostility and other negative emotions. Finally, "positive-constructive daydreaming" is most closely associated with favorable outcomes, including openness to experience and high quality of life.

Interestingly, research has shown that both night and daydreams generally reflect our conscious thought. That is, we tend to dream about what we are concerned about on a daily basis. Moreover, research has demonstrated that daydreaming helps us consolidate memories, enhance self-control, increase creativity, give us a greater sense of identity and personal meaning, and integrate ideas and plans into organized and logical wholes (Kaufman, 2004). Contrariwise, daydreaming can take our concentration away from our tasks and responsibilities at hand. It is doubtful that our teachers were impressed by the advantages of daydreaming when our minds drifted away from the work in front of us. It seems clear that there are times when we need to be focused on the external environment in order to be maximally effective. Mindfulness, an important component of ACT, allows us to be free of our internal dialogue and awareness. On the other hand, blocking out the external environment facilitates our inner workings, including the potential to daydream. Interestingly, people who tend to engage in positive daydreaming also score high in mindfulness and each promotes health and a sense of well-being. Further, mindfulness allows us to switch focus from our external to internal worlds of mental activity in flexible fashion. As Kaufman (2004) stated; "At the end of the day, these are the mental activities that make each of us unique and give our lives purpose and meaning. It is only through daydreaming that we can go beyond what is to what could be." As this author has observed over several decades of clinical practice, people rarely accomplish what they cannot imagine. Once again, it appears possible to excessively "live in the moment," to our detriment.

One final area of comment involves the use of the term Avoider. It should be made clear that this term is used to describe a process, as opposed to a stable, descriptive trait or disorder differentiating certain kinds of people. The bottom line is that we are all avoiders of pain and stress to some degree. In other words, we are different in degree rather than kind from others. As you will recall, in Chapter Two, Avoiders were referred to as having various "personality styles" based on the results of research with the MCMI. The use of personality styles was deliberate because the author did not want to convey the idea that that these types of avoidant patterns are impervious to change or somehow immutable. Certainly, some people are going to be more recalcitrant than others depending on their motivation and capacity to change, how chronic and severe the patterns are, and how much their self-defeating styles are supported by the environment. Nevertheless, if the term Avoider is conceptualized as a fixed trait-like characteristic or disorder, then there is a risk that sufferers may fuse to it. More specifically, if individuals define themselves as lowly and pathetic Avoiders, then in their minds it may seem next to impossible for them "crawl out of the hole" they find themselves in. Put another way, it is likely to be harmful if the concept of Avoider connotes a person has some type of relatively permanent disorder or disease. This type of perspective can facilitate self-fulfilling prophecies and lower the probability of constructive change. Rather, Avoiders need to accept that the patterns of avoidance that cause and/or sustain their chronic depression can change. This statement does not imply that it will be easy for them to do so. However, as pointed out previously, what in life that is easy is worthwhile? Also, we need to keep in mind a main theme of this book which is that the easy road in the short run is almost always the more difficult path in the long haul. Ultimately, we choose to live dynamically like a river or ocean or take the risk of becoming stagnant, much like a pond.

References

Aron, E. (1997). *The Highly Sensitive Person: How to Thrive When the World Overwhelms You*. Broadway Books.

Adele, & Wilson, D. (2011) Lyrics from Someone Like You. "Regrets and Mistakes They're Memories Made." Album 21. XL Recordings.

American Psychiatric Association (2013). Diagnostic and Statistical Manual of Mental Disorders (5th Ed.). Washington, DC: American Psychiatric Publishing.

Armeli, S., Temnen, H., Todd, M., Carney, M.A., Mohr, C., Affleck, G., & Hromi, A. (2003). A daily process examination of the stress-response dampening effects of alcohol consumption. *Psychology of Addictive Behaviors*, 17 (4), 266-276.

Aronson, E., Wilson, T. D., & Akert, R.M. (2013). *Social Psychology, 8th Ed*. Pearson Education, Inc.

Baumeister, R. F., Bratslavsky, Finkenauer, C., & Vohs, K. (2001); Bad is stronger than good. *Review of General Psychology, 5*: 323-70.

Beck, A. T., Rush, A., Shaw, B., & Emery, G. (1979). *Cognitive Therapy of Depression*: New York: Guilford Press.

Becker, E. (1973) *The Denial of Death*. New York, NY: The Free Press.

Begley, S.(2010). The depressing news about antidepressants. Time Magazine, February 8, 2010, pp 34-41.

Brooks, C.I., & Church, M.A. (2009). *How Psychology Applies to Everyday Life*. Santa Barbara, CA: ABC-CLIO.

Church, M.A., & Brooks, C.I. (2009). *Subtle Suicide: Our Silent Epidemic of Ambivalence About Living*. Santa Barbara, CA: ABC-CLIO.

Church, M.A., & Brooks, C.I. (2011) *The Dysfunctional Relationships of Givers and Takers: An Analysis of Toxic Chemistries*. Bloomington, ID: Author House.

Church, M.A., Kohlert, J.G., & Brooks, C.I. (2013). Relationships between MCMI-III personality patterns and depression: Analysis of 1203 tests administered in an outpatient practice. In Dr. Halkas' Psychology and the Search for Certainty. Athens Institute for Education and Research (pp. 207-216).

Covey, S. (1989). *The 7 Habits of Highly Effective People*. New York, NY: Simon and Schuster.

Dollard, J., and Miller, N.E. (1950). *Personality and Psychotherapy*. New York: McGraw-Hill.

Egan, G. (2010). *The Skilled Helper: A Problem-Management and Opportunity-Development Approach to Helping (9ᵗʰ Ed.)*. Belmont, CA: Brooks/Cole, Cengage Learning.

Frankl, V.E. (1962). *Man's Search for Meaning: An Introduction to Logotherapy*. Boston: Beacon.

Fruzzetti, A.E. (1996). Causes and consequences: Individual distress in the context of couples interactions. *Journal of Consulting and Clinical Psychology*, 64,1192-1201.

Glasser. W. Positive Addictions. New York: Harper and Row. Glasser, W. (1998) *Choice Theory: A New Psychology of Personal Freedom*. New York: Harper Collins.

Hayes, S.C., & Strosahl, K.D. *A Practical Guide to Acceptance and Commitment Therapy*, (2010). New York, NY: Springer.

Hayes, S.C. & Smith, S. (2005). *Get Out of Your Mind and Into Your Life*. Oakland, C.A.: New Harbinger Publications, Inc.

Holmes, T.H., & Rahe, R.H. (1967). The social readjustment rating scale. *Journal of Psychosomatic Research, 11*, 213-218.

Kaufman, S.B. (2014) Daydreams: How fantasies shape your future. In *Psychology Today*. April, pp. 46-55 & 80.

Kubler-Ross, E. (1969). *On Death and Dying*. New York, NY: Macmillan Publishing, Co.

Levant, R.F. (2002). We have come a long way: Psychological health care and psychophamacology. The Pennsylvania Psychologist Quarterly, November, pp. 14-15.

Locke, E.A., & Lathan, G.P. (1990). *A Theory of Goal Setting and Task Performance.* Englewood Cliffs, NJ: Prentice Hall.

Mandela, Nelson. Famous quote.

May, R. Existential model. In Sahakian, W.S. (Ed.), *Psychopathology Today: Experimentation, Theory, and Research* (1970). Itasca, IL: Peacock Publishers, Inc.

Miller, W.R., & Rollnick, S. (2002) *Motivational Interviewing. Preparing People for Change* (2nd Ed.). New York; The Guilford Press. Peele, S. The surprising truth about addiction. Psychology Today, May/June, 2004, 37, 3, pp. 43- 46.

Perls, F.S. (1976). *Gestalt Therapy Verbatim.* Bantam Book.

Robbins, A. (1991). *Awaken the Giant Within.* New York, NY: Summit Books.

Rokeach (1973). *The Nature of Human Values.* New York, NY: Free Press.

Rodgers, J.E. (2014). Go forth in anger. Psychology Today, April, pp. 92-79.

Schnarch, D. (1997). *Passionate Marriage: Keeping Love and Intimacy Alive in Committed Relationships.* New York: Henry Holt and Company, LLC.

Seligman, M.E.P., (1991). *Learned Optimism.* New York, NY: Knopf.

Sheehy, G. (1981). *Pathfinders: Overcoming the Crisis of Adult Life and Finding Your Own Path to Wellbeing.* Bantam Doubleday Dell Publishing Group.

Skinner B.F. (1974). *About Behaviorism.* New York, NY: Vintage Books.

Steinman, J. (1994). Lyrics for Meatloaf Song "Objects in the Rearview Mirror May Appear Closer than They Are." Bat Out of Hell II: Back Into Hell. MCA/Virgin.

Strosahl, K.D. (2010). ACT with the multi-problem patient. In Hayes, S.C., and Strosahl, K.D. (Eds.), *A Practical Guide to Acceptance and Commitment Therapy.* New York, NY: Springer Szalavitz, M. (2010) Antidepressants: Are they effective or just a placebo? *Time Magazine*, June, 2003.

Varra, A.A. & Follette, V.M. ACT with posttraumatic stress disorder (2010). In Hayes, S.C., & Strosahl, K.D. (Ed.), *A Practical Guide to Acceptance and Commitment Therapy*, pp 133-152, New York, NY: Springer.

Sue, P.S., Sal, D.W., & Sue, D., & Sue. S. *Understanding Abnormal Behavior* (2013), 10th Ed. Belmont, CA: Wadsworth, Cengage Learning.

Watson, D.L., & Tharp, R.G. (2007). *Self-Directed Behavior* (9th Ed.). Belmont, Calif. Thompson Higher Education.

Weinstock, C.M., & Whisman, M.A. (2006). Neuroticism as a common feature of the depressive and anxiety Disorders: A test of the revised integrative hierarchical model in a national sample. *Journal of Abnormal Psychology*, 115(1), 68-74.

Whisman, M.A., Sheldon, C.T., & Goering, P. (2000). Psychiatric disorders and dissatisfaction with social relationships. Does type matter? *Journal of Abnormal Psychology*, 109, 803-808.

Wilson, K.G., & Byrd, M.R., (2010). ACT for substance abuse and dependence. In Hayes, S.C., and Strosahl, K.D. (Ed.), *A Practical Guide to Acceptance and Commitment Therapy*, pp. 153-184, New York, NY: Springer.

Wolpe, J. (1958). *Psychotherapy by Reciprocal Inhibition*. Stanford, California: Stanford University Press.

Wood, J., Elaine Perunovic, W., and Lee, J. (2009). Positive self-statements: Power for some, peril for others. *Psychological Science*, 20(7), 860-866.

Printed in the United States
by Bookssurge, LLC

Printed in the United States
By Bookmasters